Pastries & PUFFS

Published in 2012 by ACP Books, Sydney

ACP Books are published by ACP Magazines Limited
a division of Nine Entertainment Co.

ACP BOOKS

General manager Christine Whiston
Editor-in-chief Susan Tomnay
Creative director Hieu Chi Nguyen
Art director & designer Hannah Blackmore
Senior editor Stephanie Kistner
Food director Pamela Clark
Senior food editor Rebecca Squadrito
Sales & rights director Brian Cearnes
Acting marketing manager Sonia Scali
Senior business analyst Rebecca Varela
Operations manager David Scotto
Production manager Victoria Jefferys

Published by ACP Books, a division of ACP Magazines Ltd,
54 Park St, Sydney; GPO Box 4088, Sydney, NSW 2001.
phone (02) 9282 8618; fax (02) 9126 3702.
acpbooks@acpmagazines.com.au;
www.acpbooks.com.au

To order books
phone 136 116 (within Australia) or
order online at www.acpbooks.com.au
Send recipe enquiries to:
recipeenquiries@acpmagazines.com.au

Printed in China by Everbest Printing Co Ltd.

Australia Distributed by Network Services,
phone +61 2 9282 8777; fax +61 2 9264 3278;
networkweb@networkservicescompany.com.au
New Zealand Distributed by Southern Publishers Group,
phone (9) 360 0692; fax (9) 360 0695; hub@spg.co.nz
South Africa Distributed by PSD Promotions,
phone (27 11) 392 6065/6/7; fax (27 11) 392 6079/80;
orders@psdprom.co.za

Title: Pastries and puffs / food director Pamela Clark.
ISBN: 978-1-74245-253-1 (hbk.)
Notes: Includes index.
Subjects: Pastry. Cooking. Confectionery.
Other Authors/Contributors: Clark, Pamela.
Also Titled: Australian women's weekly.
Dewey Number: 641.865

Photographer Louise Lister
Stylist Rachel Brown
Photochefs Cynthia Black, Kerrie Carr, Nicole Dicker
Recipe developer Nicole Dicker

Cover photographer Louise Lister
Cover stylist Rachel Brown
Cover photochef Nicole Dicker
Front cover (clockwise from back) Raspberry powder puffs, page 97;
Marshmallow cupcakes, page 70; Caramel éclairs, page 16; Popcake puffs,
page 24; Chouquettes (sugar puffs), page 31.
Back cover (clockwise from back) Creamy coconut cake, page 82;
Marshmallow cupcakes, page 70; Paris brest, page 11; Popcake puff, page 24;
Lemon curd and blueberry mille feuille, page 41.

*Quotes taken from *Mrs Beeton's Every Day Cookery and Housekeeping Book*,
first published by Ward, Lock & Co. Limited, 1893.

THE AUSTRALIAN
Women's Weekly

Pastries &
PUFFS

acp
books

CONTENTS

The art of making pastry requires much practice, dexterity and skill: it should be touched as lightly as possible, made with cool hands and in a cool place.

– Mrs Beeton's Every Day Cookery, 1893

Puffs &
Profiteroles

CLASSIC PUFFS

½ cup (125ml) water
60g (2 ounces) butter,
   chopped finely
1 tablespoon caster (superfine)
   sugar
½ cup (75g) strong baker's flour
3 eggs
1 tablespoon icing
   (confectioners') sugar
crème pâtissière
3 cups (750ml) milk
⅔ cup (150g) caster (superfine)
   sugar
1 teaspoon vanilla extract
⅓ cup (50g) cornflour
   (cornstarch)
6 egg yolks

1 Make crème pâtissière.
2 Preheat oven to 220°C/425°F.
Grease oven trays.
3 To make choux pastry, combine
the water, butter and caster
sugar in medium saucepan; bring
to the boil (see page 120). Add
flour, beat with wooden spoon
over heat until mixture comes
away from base of pan (see page
120). Transfer pastry to medium
bowl; beat in two of the eggs,
one at a time (see page 120).
Whisk remaining egg with a fork,
beat enough of the egg into the
pastry until it becomes smooth
and glossy but will hold its shape
(see page 120).
4 Drop level tablespoons of
pastry, about 5cm (2 inches)
apart, on trays (see page 120).
5 Bake puffs 10 minutes. Reduce
oven to 180°C/350°F; bake
15 minutes. Cut small opening in
base of each puff; bake further
10 minutes or until puffs are dry.
Cool on trays.

6 Spoon crème pâtissière into
piping bag fitted with 5mm
(¼-inch) plain tube; pipe through
cuts into puffs (see page 120).
Dust puffs with sifted icing sugar.
crème pâtissière Combine milk,
sugar and extract in medium
saucepan; bring to the boil.
Meanwhile, whisk cornflour with
egg yolks in medium heatproof
bowl; gradually whisk in hot milk
mixture. Return mixture to pan;
stir over heat until mixture boils
and thickens. Cover surface of
crème pâtissière with plastic
wrap. Refrigerate 4 hours.

prep + cook time
1 hour 10 minutes
(+ cooling & refrigeration)
makes 20

PARIS BREST

½ cup (125ml) water
60g (2 ounces) butter, chopped finely
1 tablespoon caster (superfine) sugar
½ cup (75g) strong baker's flour
3 eggs
2 tablespoons flaked almonds
1 tablespoon icing (confectioners') sugar
praline cream
⅓ cup (75g) caster (superfine) sugar
2 tablespoons water
⅓ cup (25g) flaked almonds, roasted
2 cups (500ml) thickened (heavy) cream, whipped

1 Preheat oven to 220°C/425°F. Grease oven trays.
2 To make choux pastry, combine the water, butter and caster sugar in medium saucepan; bring to the boil (see page 120). Add flour, beat with wooden spoon over heat until mixture comes away from base of pan (see page 120). Transfer pastry to medium bowl; beat in two of the eggs, one at a time (see page 120). Whisk remaining egg with a fork, beat enough of the egg into the pastry until it becomes smooth and glossy but will hold its shape (see page 120).
3 Spoon pastry into piping bag fitted with 1.5cm (¾-inch) fluted tube; pipe 5.5cm (2¼-inch) rings, about 5cm (2 inches) apart on trays (see page 120). Sprinkle top with nuts.
4 Bake rings 10 minutes. Reduce oven to 180°C/350°F; bake 15 minutes. Using serrated knife, split rings in half, remove any soft centres; return to trays, bake further 5 minutes or until puffs are dry. Cool on trays.

5 Meanwhile, make praline cream.
6 Spread cream into pastry bases; top with pastry tops. Dust with sifted icing sugar.
praline cream Line tray with baking paper. Stir sugar and the water in small saucepan over high heat, without boiling, until sugar dissolves. Bring to the boil. Boil, uncovered, without stirring, until golden brown. Allow bubbles to subside; add nuts; do not stir. Pour mixture onto tray; leave praline to set at room temperature. Break praline into pieces, then process until fine; fold into whipped cream.

prep + cook time
1 hour 10 minutes
makes 12

DOUBLE CHOCOLATE PUFFS

½ cup (125ml) water
60g (2 ounces) butter, chopped finely
1 tablespoon caster (superfine) sugar
½ cup (75g) strong baker's flour
2 tablespoons cocoa powder
3 eggs
1 cup (250ml) thickened (heavy) cream, whipped

chocolate mousse
90g (3 ounces) dark eating (semi-sweet) chocolate, chopped coarsely
⅔ cup (160ml) thickened (heavy) cream
1 egg, separated
1 tablespoon caster (superfine) sugar

1 Make chocolate mousse.
2 Preheat oven to 220°C/425°F. Grease oven trays.
3 To make choux pastry, combine the water, butter and sugar in medium saucepan; bring to the boil (see page 120). Add sifted flour and cocoa, beat with wooden spoon over heat until mixture comes away from base of pan (see page 120). Transfer pastry to medium bowl; beat in two of the eggs, one at a time (see page 120). Whisk remaining egg with a fork, beat enough of the egg into the pastry until it becomes smooth and glossy but will hold its shape (see page 120).
4 Drop rounded tablespoons of pastry, about 5cm (2 inches) apart, on trays (see page 120).
5 Bake puffs 10 minutes. Reduce oven to 180°C/350°F; bake 15 minutes. Using serrated knife, split puffs in half, remove any soft centres; return to trays, bake further 5 minutes or until puffs are dry. Cool on trays.

6 Spoon chocolate mousse into piping bag fitted with 1.5cm (¾-inch) fluted tube; pipe mousse into pastry bases (see page 120). Top with whipped cream then pastry tops. Dust with a little extra sifted cocoa.

chocolate mousse Place chocolate and half the cream in medium heatproof bowl over a medium saucepan of simmering water; stir until smooth. Cool mixture 5 minutes, then stir in egg yolk. Beat remaining cream in small bowl with electric mixer until soft peaks form. Beat egg white in another small bowl with electric mixer until soft peaks form; add sugar, beat until sugar dissolves. Fold cream into chocolate mixture, then fold in egg white. Cover; refrigerate overnight.

prep + cook time
1 hour 20 minutes (+ refrigeration)
makes 10

MARBLED RASPBERRY MASCARPONE PUFFS

½ cup (125ml) water
60g (2 ounces) butter,
  chopped finely
1 tablespoon caster (superfine)
  sugar
½ cup (75g) strong baker's flour
3 eggs
200g (6½ ounces) fresh
  raspberries

mascarpone cream
250g (8 ounces) cream cheese,
  softened
250g (8 ounces) mascarpone
  cheese
1 cup (250ml) thick (double)
  cream
½ cup (160g) raspberry jam

raspberry glacé icing
50g (1½ ounces) fresh
  raspberries
1 cup (160g) icing
  (confectioners') sugar
10g (½ ounce) soft butter
1 teaspoon hot water,
  approximately

1 Preheat oven to 220°C/425°F. Grease oven trays.
2 To make choux pastry, combine the water, butter and sugar in medium saucepan; bring to the boil (see page 120). Add flour, beat with wooden spoon over heat until mixture comes away from base of pan (see page 120). Transfer pastry to medium bowl; beat in two of the eggs, one at a time (see page 120). Whisk remaining egg with a fork, beat enough of the egg into the pastry until it becomes smooth and glossy but will hold its shape (see page 120).
3 Drop level tablespoons of pastry, about 5cm (2-inch) apart, on trays (see page 120).
4 Bake 10 minutes. Reduce oven to 180°C/350°F; bake 15 minutes. Using serrated knife, split puffs in half, remove any soft centres; return to trays, bake further 5 minutes or until puffs are dry. Cool on trays.

5 Meanwhile, make mascarpone cream and raspberry glacé icing.
6 Spoon mascarpone cream into pastry bases; top with pastry tops. Drizzle puffs with icing, top with raspberries.

mascarpone cream Beat cream cheese and mascarpone in small bowl with electric mixer until smooth. Fold in cream, then jam for marbled effect.

raspberry glacé icing Push raspberries through fine sieve into small heatproof bowl; discard seeds. Sift icing sugar into bowl with raspberry puree; stir in butter and enough of the water to make a thick paste. Place bowl over small saucepan of simmering water; stir until icing is spreadable.

prep + cook time
1 hour 15 minutes
makes 20

CARAMEL ECLAIRS

395g (12½ ounces) sweetened
    condensed milk
½ cup (125ml) water
60g (2 ounces) butter,
    chopped finely
1 tablespoon dark brown sugar
½ cup (75g) strong baker's flour
3 eggs
2 cups (500ml) thickened (heavy)
    cream, whipped
caramel icing
30g (1 ounce) butter,
    chopped coarsely
¼ cup (55g) firmly packed
    dark brown sugar
1 tablespoon milk
⅓ cup (55g) icing
    (confectioners') sugar

1 Preheat oven to 220°C/425°F.
2 Pour condensed milk into
medium shallow baking dish;
cover with foil. Place dish in
large baking dish; add enough
boiling water to large dish to
come halfway up sides of dish.
Bake, uncovered, about 1¼ hours
or until condensed milk is golden
brown and caramel. Cool to room
temperature. Whisk caramel
until smooth.
3 To make choux pastry, combine
the water, butter and sugar in
medium saucepan; bring to the
boil (see page 120). Add flour,
beat with wooden spoon over
heat until mixture comes away
from base of pan (see page 120).
Transfer pastry to medium bowl;
beat in two of the eggs, one at
a time (see page 120). Whisk
remaining egg with a fork, beat
enough of the egg into the
pastry until it becomes smooth
and glossy but will hold its shape
(see page 120).
4 Spoon pastry into piping bag
fitted with 1.5cm (¾-inch) plain
tube. Pipe 8cm (3-inch) lengths,
about 5cm (2 inches) apart, on
greased oven trays.

5 Bake éclairs 10 minutes.
Reduce oven to 180°C/350°F;
bake 15 minutes. Using serrated
knife, cut éclairs in half, remove
any soft centres; return to trays,
bake further 5 minutes or until
éclairs are dry. Cool on trays.
6 Meanwhile, make caramel
icing.
7 Spoon cream into pastry
bases, top with caramel.
Position pastry tops on bases;
spread with caramel icing.
caramel icing Melt butter in
small saucepan. Add brown
sugar and milk; cook, stirring,
over heat, without boiling, until
sugar dissolves. Bring to the boil.
Reduce heat; simmer, uncovered,
1 minute. Remove from heat;
cool 10 minutes. Whisk in sifted
icing sugar.

prep + cook time
2 hours 15 minutes (+ cooling)
makes 18

BERRY PUFF CHEESECAKE

1½ cups (375ml) water
125g (4 ounces) butter,
  chopped finely
1 tablespoon caster
  (superfine) sugar
1½ cups (225g) strong
  baker's flour
6 eggs
½ cup (40g) flaked almonds,
  roasted
2 teaspoons icing
  (confectioners') sugar
berry cheesecake filling
1kg (2 pounds) cream cheese,
  softened
2 teaspoons vanilla extract
1 cup (220g) caster
  (superfine) sugar
3 cups (750ml) thickened
  (heavy) cream
250g (8 ounces) fresh
  blueberries
125g (4 ounces) fresh
  raspberries, halved

1 Preheat oven to 220°C/425°F. Grease three oven trays. Trace a 20cm (8-inch) round onto three sheets baking paper to use as a guide; line trays with paper, marked-side down.

2 To make choux pastry, combine the water, butter and caster sugar in medium saucepan; bring to the boil (see page 120). Add flour, beat with wooden spoon over heat until mixture comes away from base of pan (see page 120). Transfer pastry to medium bowl; beat in eggs, one at a time, until pastry becomes glossy (see page 120).

3 Spoon pastry into piping bag fitted with 1.5cm (¾-inch) fluted tube. Pipe pastry into a spiral on each tray, using paper as a guide (see page 120).

4 Bake pastry 10 minutes. Reduce oven to 180°C/350°F; bake further 45 minutes or until dry. Cool on trays.

5 Meanwhile, make berry cheesecake filling.

6 Place one pastry round on serving plate; top with half the filling. Top with another pastry round and remaining filling. Top with remaining pastry round. Spread reserved filling around side of cake; press nuts around side of cake. Cover; refrigerate 2 hours. Serve cake topped with extra berries and dusted with sifted icing sugar.

berry cheesecake filling Beat cream cheese, extract and sugar in large bowl with electric mixer until smooth; gradually beat in cream. Reserve 2 cups of cheesecake filling; fold berries into remaining mixture.

prep + cook time
1 hour 40 minutes (+ refrigeration)
serves 16
tip Use a serrated knife to cut the cake

VALENTINE'S CROQUEMBOUCHE

⅓ cup (80ml) water
40g (1½ ounces) butter, chopped finely
3 teaspoons caster (superfine) sugar
⅓ cup (50g) strong baker's flour
2 eggs

strawberries & cream custard
1 cup (250ml) milk
2 tablespoons caster (superfine) sugar
1½ tablespoons cornflour (cornstarch)
2 egg yolks
30g (1 ounce) strawberries, chopped finely
1 teaspoon icing (confectioners') sugar

toffee
1 cup (220g) caster (superfine) sugar
½ cup (125ml) water

chocolate fondue
½ cup (125ml) pouring cream
100g (3 ounces) dark eating (semi-sweet) chocolate, chopped finely

1 Make strawberries & cream custard.
2 Preheat oven to 220°C/425°F. Grease oven trays.
3 To make choux pastry, combine the water, butter and sugar in medium saucepan; bring to the boil (see page 120). Add flour, beat with wooden spoon over heat until mixture comes away from base of pan (see page 120). Transfer pastry to medium bowl; beat in eggs, one at a time, until pastry becomes glossy (see page 120).
4 Spoon pastry into piping bag fitted with 1cm (½-inch) plain tube. Pipe 2cm (¾-inch) rounds onto trays (see page 121).
5 Bake 10 minutes. Reduce oven to 180°C/350°F; bake 10 minutes. Cut small opening in base of each puff; bake further 10 minutes or until puffs are dry. Cool on trays.
6 Spoon custard into piping bag fitted with 5mm (¼-inch) plain tube; pipe through cuts into puffs (see page 120).
7 Make toffee, then make chocolate fondue.
8 To assemble croquembouche, carefully dip puffs, one at a time, into toffee (see page 121); arrange 10 puffs on serving plate in ring shape. Fill centre of ring with more puffs. Continue dipping and stacking puffs to make a cone shape (see page 121).

9 Working quickly, dip fork into remaining toffee and lightly drizzle toffee all over croquembouche (see page 121). Serve croquembouche with chocolate fondue and sprinkle with rose petals, if you like.

strawberries & cream custard Bring milk and sugar to the boil in medium saucepan. Meanwhile, combine cornflour and egg yolks in medium heatproof bowl; gradually whisk in hot milk mixture. Return mixture to pan; stir over heat until custard boils and thickens. Cover surface of custard with plastic wrap; cool 20 minutes. Refrigerate 4 hours. Meanwhile, combine strawberries and icing sugar in small bowl. Cover; refrigerate 1 hour. Fold strawberry mixture, into custard.

toffee Stir sugar and the water in small saucepan over heat, without boiling, until sugar dissolves. Bring to the boil; boil, uncovered, without stirring, until golden brown.

chocolate fondue Bring cream to the boil in small saucepan. Remove from heat; add chocolate, stir until smooth.

prep + cook time
1 hour 30 minutes (+ refrigeration)
serves 2
tip You might have a few puffs left over; freeze them, unfilled.

GATEAU ST HONORE

2 sheets puff pastry
⅓ cup (80ml) water
40g (1½ ounces) butter,
   chopped finely
3 teaspoons caster (superfine)
   sugar
⅓ cup (50g) strong baker's flour
2 eggs
250g (8 ounces) strawberries,
   quartered
100g (3 ounces) white eating
   chocolate, melted
crème pâtissière
1 vanilla bean
1½ cups (375ml) milk
⅔ cup (150g) caster (superfine)
   sugar
⅓ cup (50g) pure cornflour
   (cornstarch)
6 egg yolks
⅓ cup (80ml) thickened (heavy)
   cream, whipped
toffee
1 cup (220g) caster (superfine)
   sugar
½ cup (125ml) water

1 Make crème pâtissière.
2 Preheat oven to 220°C/425°F.
Grease oven trays.
3 Brush one puff pastry sheet
with a little water; top with
remaining pastry, press firmly.
Cut 20cm (8-inch) round from
pastry stack. Place pastry on tray;
prick well with fork.
4 To make choux pastry, combine
the water, butter and sugar in small
saucepan; bring to the boil (see
page 120). Add flour, beat with
wooden spoon over heat until
mixture comes away from base
of pan (see page 120). Transfer
pastry to medium bowl; beat in
eggs, one at a time, until pastry
becomes glossy (see page 120).
5 Spoon choux pastry into piping
bag fitted with 1.5cm (¾-inch)
plain tube, pipe around edge of
puff pastry round (see page 121).
Pipe 3.5cm (1½-inch) rounds of
choux pastry, about 5cm (2-inch)
apart, on another tray.
6 Bake both trays 10 minutes.
Reduce oven to 180°C/350°F;
bake further 30 minutes. Cool
on trays.
7 Meanwhile, make toffee.
8 Make small cut in each puff.
Spoon crème pâtissière into
piping bag fitted with 5mm
(¼-inch) plain tube; pipe through
cuts into puffs (see page 120).
Spoon remaining crème
pâtissière into centre of gateau
(see page 121).

9 Dip puffs, one at a time, in
toffee (see page 121); place
around edge on gateau (see
page 121). Fill gateau with
strawberries. Drizzle strawberries
with chocolate. Working quickly,
dip fork into remaining toffee,
drizzle toffee all over gateau
(see page 121).

crème pâtissière Split vanilla
bean; scrape seeds into milk
and sugar in small saucepan,
discard bean. Bring to the boil.
Meanwhile, combine cornflour
and egg yolks in medium
heatproof bowl; gradually whisk
in hot milk mixture. Return
custard to pan; stir over heat
until mixture boils and thickens.
Cover surface of custard with
plastic wrap; cool 20 minutes.
Refrigerate 3 hours. Fold cream
into custard, in two batches.
Cover; refrigerate until ready
to use.

toffee Stir sugar and the water
in small saucepan over heat,
without boiling, until sugar
dissolves. Bring to the boil;
boil, uncovered, without stirring,
until golden brown.

prep + cook time
2 hours 20 minutes (+ refrigeration)
serves 8

POPCAKE PUFFS

⅓ cup (80ml) water
40g (1½ ounces) butter, chopped finely
3 teaspoons caster (superfine) sugar
⅓ cup (50g) strong baker's flour
2 eggs

crème pâtissière
1⅓ cups (330ml) milk
⅓ cup (75g) caster (superfine) sugar
1 teaspoon vanilla extract
2 tablespoons cornflour (cornstarch)
3 egg yolks

toffee
2 cups (440g) caster (superfine) sugar
1 cup (250ml) water

1 Make crème pâtissière.

2 Preheat oven to 220°C/425°F. Grease oven trays.

3 To make choux pastry, combine the water, butter and sugar in small saucepan; bring to the boil (see page 120). Add flour, beat with wooden spoon over heat until mixture comes away from base of pan (see page 120). Transfer pastry to medium bowl; beat in eggs, one at a time, until pastry becomes glossy (see page 120).

4 Drop rounded teaspoons of pastry, about 5cm (2 inches) apart, on trays (see page 120).

5 Bake puffs 10 minutes. Reduce oven to 180°C/350°F; bake 15 minutes. Cut small opening in base of each puff; bake further 10 minutes or until puffs are dry. Cool on trays.

6 Spoon crème pâtissière into piping bag fitted with 3mm (⅛-inch) plain tube; pipe through cuts into puffs (see page 120).

7 Make toffee.

8 Push one paddle pop stick into each puff. Working quickly, dip puffs in toffee; place on baking-paper-lined oven tray. Stand at room temperature until set.

crème pâtissière Combine milk, sugar and extract in small saucepan; bring to the boil. Meanwhile, combine cornflour and egg yolks in medium heatproof bowl; gradually whisk in hot milk mixture. Return mixture to pan; stir over heat until custard boils and thickens. Cover surface of custard with plastic wrap; cool 20 minutes. Refrigerate 4 hours.

toffee Stir sugar and the water in medium saucepan over heat, without boiling, until sugar dissolves. Bring to the boil; boil, uncovered, without stirring, until small amount of toffee dropped into cold water sets hard and can be snapped with fingers.

prep + cook time
1 hour 30 minutes (+ refrigeration)
makes 34
tips You will need 17 paddle pop sticks (halved) for this recipe. When dipping the puff popcakes in toffee, tilt the pan of toffee to one side, so the toffee is deep enough to completely coat the popcakes and a bit of the stick in toffee; this will ensure the popcakes don't fall off the sticks.

LEMON CREAM PUFFS

½ cup (125ml) water
60g (2 ounces) butter,
  chopped finely
1 tablespoon caster (superfine)
  sugar
½ cup (75g) strong baker's flour
3 eggs
lemon cream filling
2 cups (500ml) milk
3 teaspoons finely grated
  lemon rind
6 egg yolks
½ cup (110g) caster (superfine)
  sugar
⅓ cup (50g) cornflour
  (cornstarch)
1 cup (250ml) thick (double)
  cream
lemon icing
1 cup (160g) pure icing
  (confectioners') sugar
2 teaspoons lemon juice,
  approximately

1 Make lemon cream filling.
2 Preheat oven to 220°C/425°F. Grease oven trays.
3 To make choux pastry, combine the water, butter and sugar in small saucepan; bring to the boil (see page 120). Add flour, beat with wooden spoon over heat until mixture comes away from base of pan (see page 120). Transfer pastry to medium bowl; beat in two of the eggs, one at a time (see page 120). Whisk remaining egg with a fork, beat enough of the egg into the pastry until it becomes smooth and glossy but will hold its shape (see page 120).
4 Drop level tablespoons of pastry, about 5cm (2 inches) apart, on trays (see page 120).
5 Bake 10 minutes. Reduce oven to 180°C/350°F; bake 15 minutes. Cut small opening in base of puff; bake further 10 minutes or until puffs are dry. Cool on trays.
6 Make lemon icing.
7 Spoon filling into piping bag fitted with 5mm (¼-inch) plain tube; pipe through cuts into puffs (see page 120). Place puffs on foil-covered tray; drizzle with lemon icing.

lemon cream filling Bring milk to the boil in medium saucepan. Meanwhile, combine rind, egg yolks, sugar and cornflour in medium heatproof bowl; gradually whisk in hot milk. Return custard to pan; stir over heat until mixture boils and thickens. Cover surface of custard with plastic wrap; cool 20 minutes. Refrigerate 3 hours. Fold in cream, in two batches.
lemon icing Sift icing sugar into small heatproof bowl. Stir in enough lemon juice to make a stiff paste. Stir icing over small saucepan of simmering water until spreadable.

prep + cook time
1 hour 20 minutes (+ refrigeration)
makes 20
tip To make candied lemon strips: remove the rind from one lemon, using a zester. Drop the rind into a small saucepan of boiling water; drain. Do this two more times. Toss rind in a little caster (superfine) sugar; cool.

CLASSIC CHOCOLATE ECLAIRS

1 cup (250ml) water
125g (4 ounces) butter,
 chopped finely
2 tablespoons caster (superfine)
 sugar
1 cup (150g) strong baker's flour
6 eggs
chocolate pastry cream
2 cups (500ml) milk
150g (4½ ounces) dark eating
 (semi-sweet) chocolate,
 chopped coarsely
2 tablespoons dutch cocoa
 powder
5 egg yolks
½ cup (110g) caster (superfine)
 sugar
⅓ cup (50g) cornflour
 (cornstarch)
50g (1½ ounces) butter,
 chopped coarsely
chocolate glaze
80g (2½ ounces) dark eating
 (semi-sweet) chocolate,
 chopped coarsely
80g (2½ ounces) milk eating
 chocolate, chopped coarsely
40g (1½ ounces) butter

1 Make chocolate pastry cream.
2 Preheat oven to 220°C/425°F.
Grease two oven trays.
3 To make choux pastry, combine
the water, butter and sugar in
medium saucepan; bring to the
boil (see page 120). Add flour,
stir over heat until mixture comes
away from base of pan (see page
120). Transfer pastry to medium
bowl; beat in eggs, one at a time,
until pastry becomes glossy (see
page 120).
4 Spoon pastry into piping bag
fitted with 1.5cm (¾-inch) plain
tube. Pipe 10cm (4-inch) lengths,
about 5cm (2 inches) apart,
on trays.
5 Bake éclairs about 20 minutes
or until golden and puffed;
transfer to wire rack to cool.
Cut éclairs in half, remove any
soft centres; return to the oven
for about 5 minutes to dry out
if necessary.
6 Make chocolate glaze.
7 Spoon pastry cream into
piping bag fitted with 1.5cm
(¾-inch) fluted tube; pipe into
bottoms of éclairs. Place on wire
rack; replace tops, spread with
chocolate glaze.

chocolate pastry cream
Combine milk, chocolate and
sifted cocoa in small saucepan;
stir over medium heat until
smooth. Bring to the boil.
Meanwhile, whisk egg yolks,
sugar and cornflour in medium
heatproof bowl until smooth.
Gradually whisk in hot milk
mixture. Strain custard into
medium saucepan; whisk over
medium heat until mixture boils
and thickens. Remove from heat;
whisk in butter until smooth.
Transfer pastry cream to medium
bowl, cover surface with plastic
wrap; refrigerate 2 hours.
chocolate glaze Stir ingredients
in small heatproof bowl over small
saucepan of simmering water
until smooth. Use while warm.

prep + cook time
1 hour 15 minutes (+ refrigeration
& cooling) **makes** 12
tips Chocolate and coffee
éclairs are found in every bakery
in France. The origin of their
name, éclair (meaning lightning)
is unknown. It could be that they
are so delicious they are eaten in
a flash or it could come from the
shine of the glaze. Dutch cocoa
powder is a richly flavoured dark
coloured cocoa. It's available in
delis and specialist food stores.

CHOUQUETTES (SUGAR PUFFS)

½ cup (125ml) water
60g (2 ounces) butter
1 tablespoon caster (superfine)
  sugar
½ cup (75g) strong baker's flour
4 eggs
¼ cup (45g) pearl sugar

1 Preheat oven to 220°C/425°F. Grease two oven trays.
2 To make choux pastry, combine the water, butter and caster sugar in small saucepan; bring to the boil (see page 120). Add flour, stir over heat until mixture comes away from base and side of pan and forms a smooth ball (see page 120). Transfer dough to medium bowl; beat in three of the eggs, one at a time, until dough becomes smooth and glossy (see page 120).
3 Spoon pastry into piping bag fitted with 1cm (½-inch) plain tube. Pipe small rounds, about 5cm (2 inches) apart, on trays; brush all over with lightly beaten remaining egg, sprinkle with pearl sugar.
4 Bake puffs about 20 minutes or until golden and puffed. Serve warm.

prep + cook time 30 minutes
makes 40
tips These puffs are best eaten soon after baking. They are a traditional French afternoon snack for kids after school. They are sold at bakeries by the weight in paper bags. Pearl sugar is a coarse white sugar which keeps its shape when heated or exposed to moisture; it's available at specialist food stores.

PASSIONFRUIT RASPBERRY ECLAIRS

½ cup (125ml) water

60g (2 ounces) butter

1 tablespoon caster (superfine) sugar

½ cup (75g) strong baker's flour

3 eggs

1 cup (250ml) thickened (heavy) cream

1 tablespoon pure icing (confectioner's) sugar

3 passionfruit, halved

⅓ cup (40g) fresh raspberries

1 cup (160g) pure icing (confectioner's) sugar, extra

1 Preheat oven to 220°C/425°F. Grease two oven trays.

2 To make choux pastry, combine the water, butter and caster sugar in small saucepan; bring to the boil (see page 120). Add flour, beat with wooden spoon over heat until mixture comes away from base of pan (see page 120). Transfer pastry to medium bowl; beat in two of the eggs, one at a time (see page 120). Whisk remaining egg with a fork, beat enough of the egg into the pastry until it becomes smooth and glossy but will hold its shape (see page 120).

3 Spoon pastry into piping bag fitted with 1.5 cm (¾-inch) plain tube. Pipe 8cm (3¼-inch) lengths, about 5cm (2 inches) apart, on trays.

4 Bake éclairs about 20 minutes or until golden and puffed. Cool on wire rack.

5 Meanwhile, beat cream and sifted icing sugar in medium bowl with electric mixer until firm peaks form; stir in 2 tablespoons of passionfruit pulp and lightly crushed raspberries; refrigerate.

6 To make passionfruit icing, strain remaining passionfruit pulp (you need about 1 tablespoon); discard seeds. Sift extra icing sugar into small heatproof bowl; stir in enough passionfruit juice to make a thick paste. Place bowl over small saucepan of simmering water; stir until mixture is smooth and spreadable.

7 Using serrated knife, cut éclairs in half. Spoon passionfruit cream into bases, top with pastry tops. Spread icing over éclairs.

prep + cook time
40 minutes (+ cooling)
makes 14

So many pretty dishes of pastry may be made by stamping puff-paste out with fancy cutters... and by exercising a little ingenuity, variety may be obtained.

– Mrs Beeton's Every Day Cookery, 1893*

Pastries &
TARTS

MINI APPLE TARTE TATINS

1 cup (150g) strong baker's flour
150g (4½ ounces) butter,
   at room temperature,
   chopped coarsely
⅔ cup (160ml) iced water,
   approximately
¼ cup (60ml) thick (double)
   cream
caramelised apple
3 small apples (390g)
2 tablespoons lemon juice
½ cup (110g) caster (superfine)
   sugar
50g (1½ ounces) unsalted
   butter, chopped coarsely
2 tablespoons water

1 To make pastry, sift flour into medium bowl; rub in butter until mixture is crumbly and you can still see small chunks of butter. Make a well in the centre. Stir in enough of the water to make firm dough. Knead dough on floured surface until smooth; shape into rectangle. Wrap pastry in plastic; refrigerate 20 minutes.

2 Roll pastry on floured surface into 20cm x 40cm (8-inch x 16-inch) rectangle, keeping edges straight and even. Fold the top third of pastry down until two-thirds of the way down the rectangle, then fold the bottom third up and over (see page 122). Turn the dough a quarter-turn clockwise; repeat rolling and folding once more (see page 122). Wrap pastry in plastic; refrigerate 1 hour.

3 Meanwhile, make caramelised apple.

4 Roll pastry on floured surface until 3mm (⅛-inch) thick. Cut 12 x 6cm (2½-inch) rounds from pastry. Place rounds on top of apples in pan, tuck pastry down side of pan holes.

5 Bake tarts about 30 minutes. Stand tarts in pan 20 minutes before turning onto baking-paper-lined tray. Serve topped with cream.

caramelised apple Preheat oven to 200°C/400°F; grease 12-hole (1½-tablespoon/30ml) shallow round-based patty pan. Peel, core and quarter apples; slice thinly, without cutting through the apple (see page 122). Combine apples and juice in medium bowl. Stir sugar, butter and half the water in small frying pan, over heat, without boiling, until sugar dissolves. Bring to the boil. Reduce heat; simmer, uncovered, without stirring, about 8 minutes, shaking pan occasionally, until dark caramel in colour. Allow bubbles to subside, then carefully spoon caramel into pan holes. Add the remaining water to hot frying pan; reserve caramel liquid. Position one apple quarter, trimmed to fit, rounded-side down, in each pan hole; brush apples with reserved caramel liquid. Cover patty pan with foil, place on oven tray; bake 10 minutes. Remove foil.

prep + cook time
1 hour 20 minutes (+ refrigeration & standing) **makes** 12
tips The butter should be at room temperature but not soft. Leftover trimmings of pastry should be stacked up and chilled for another use. Don't press scraps together in a ball as the flaky layers of pastry will be spoiled.

CHERRY ALMOND TARTLETS

90g (3 ounces) unsalted butter, softened
2 tablespoons caster (superfine) sugar
1 egg yolk
1 cup (150g) plain (all-purpose) flour
½ cup (60g) ground almonds
1 tablespoon black cherry jam
12 fresh cherries with stems (150g)
almond filling
125g (4 ounces) unsalted butter, softened
½ teaspoon finely grated lemon rind
½ cup (110g) caster (superfine) sugar
2 eggs
¾ cup (90g) ground almonds
2 tablespoons plain (all-purpose) flour

1 Beat butter, sugar and egg yolk in small bowl with electric mixer until combined. Stir in sifted flour and ground almonds, in two batches. Turn dough onto floured surface; knead until smooth. Roll pastry between sheets of baking paper until 3mm (⅛-inch) thick; place on tray. Refrigerate 30 minutes.
2 Preheat oven to 220°C/425°F. Grease 12-hole (1½-tablespoon/ 30ml) shallow round-based patty pan.
3 Make almond filling.
4 Cut 12 x 6.5cm (2½-inch) rounds from pastry; press rounds into pan holes. Divide jam between pastry cases, spoon filling into cases, place a cherry in the centre of the filling.
5 Bake tartlets about 20 minutes. Stand tartlets in pan 10 minutes before turning, top-side up, onto wire rack.

almond filling Beat butter, rind and sugar in small bowl with electric mixer until light and fluffy. Beat in eggs, one at a time. Stir in ground almonds and flour.

prep + cook time
55 minutes (+ refrigeration)
makes 12
tip If cherries are out of season you could use 425g (13½ ounces) canned seedless black cherries; drain cherries well on absorbent paper before using.

LEMON CURD & BLUEBERRY MILLE FEUILLE

3 sheets fillo pastry
1 egg white, beaten lightly
¼ cup (40g) icing
   (confectioners') sugar
185g (6 ounces) ghee
500g (1 pound) blueberries
lemon curd
2 egg yolks
¼ cup (55g) caster (superfine)
   sugar
1 teaspoon finely grated
   lemon rind
2 tablespoons lemon juice
60g (2 ounces) cold unsalted
   butter, chopped coarsely

1 Make lemon curd.
2 Brush one sheet of pastry with a little of the egg white; top with remaining two pastry sheets, brushing between each with more egg white. Cut 18 x 4cm x 10cm (1½-inch x 4-inch) rectangles from pastry. Dust both sides of rectangles with 2 tablespoons of the sifted icing sugar.
3 Heat ghee in medium frying pan; cook pastry, in batches, until browned lightly and crisp. Drain on absorbent paper.
4 Drop one teaspoon of lemon curd onto centre of six serving plates; top each with one pastry piece. Divide half the lemon curd and half the berries over pastry. Top each with another pastry piece, then remaining curd and berries; top with remaining pastry. Serve dusted with remaining sifted icing sugar.

lemon curd Whisk egg yolks and sugar in small heatproof bowl until pale and thickened slightly. Whisk in rind and juice; stir over small saucepan of simmering water 12 minutes or until mixture coats the back of a spoon. Remove from heat; gradually whisk in butter until combined between additions (see page 121). Cool.

prep + cook time
1 hour 10 minutes (+ refrigeration)
makes 6
tip Ghee, also called clarified butter is available from the refrigerated section of large supermarkets. To make clarified butter, place 185g (6 ounces) of unsalted butter in small saucepan; melt butter over low heat until it separates into three layers. Remove saucepan from heat and stand 5 minutes. Skim off the top layer of white foam (the whey proteins) and discard. The milk solids will drop to the bottom of the saucepan and form a milky layer of sediment. What's left in the middle is clarified butter. Strain the mixture through muslin-lined sieve and discard milk solids.

FIG CUSTARD PASTRIES

3 sheets butter puff pastry
5 medium fresh figs (300g),
  halved, sliced thinly
¼ cup (55g) firmly packed
  light brown sugar
crème pâtissière
1 cup (250ml) milk
⅓ cup (75g) caster (superfine)
  sugar
1 teaspoon vanilla extract
2 tablespoons cornflour
  (cornstarch)
3 egg yolks
2 tablespoons thick (double)
  cream

1 Make crème pâtissière.
2 Meanwhile, preheat oven to
200°C/425°F. Grease oven trays.
3 Brush one pastry sheet lightly
with water; top with another
sheet, press firmly. Cut 16 x
5.5cm (2¼-inch) rounds from
pastry stack; cut 3.5cm (1½-inch)
rounds from centre of each
round, discard small rounds.
4 Cut 16 x 5.5cm (2¼-inch)
rounds from remaining pastry
sheet; place on oven trays, brush
lightly with water. Top rounds
with pastry rings, press gently.
5 Bake about 30 minutes.
Cool on trays.
6 Preheat grill (broiler).
7 Using teaspoon press down
centre of cases; spoon crème
pâtissière into cases. Top with
fig slices; sprinkle figs with sugar.
Grill until sugar caramelises.

crème pâtissière Bring milk,
sugar and extract to the boil
in small saucepan. Meanwhile,
combine cornflour and egg yolks
in medium heatproof bowl;
gradually whisk in hot milk
mixture. Return mixture to pan;
stir over heat until custard boils
and thickens. Cover surface of
custard with plastic wrap; cool
20 minutes. Refrigerate 2 hours.
Fold in cream.

prep + cook time
1 hour 20 minutes (+ refrigeration)
makes 16

APRICOT PASTRIES

2 sheets butter puff pastry
1kg (2 pounds) canned apricot
  halves in natural juice, drained
1 egg, beaten lightly
½ cup (160g) apricot jam,
  warmed, strained
crème pâtissière
⅔ cup (160ml) milk
¼ cup (55g) caster (superfine)
  sugar
1 teaspoon vanilla extract
1 tablespoon cornflour
  (cornstarch)
2 egg yolks

1 Make crème pâtissière.
2 Preheat oven to 180°C/350°F.
Grease and line two oven trays
with baking paper.
3 Cut 9 x 7cm (2¾-inch) rounds
from each sheet of pastry; place
on trays. Use a 5cm (2-inch)
cutter to mark a ring on each
round of pastry; do not cut all
the way through (see page 122).
4 Drop a level teaspoon of
crème pâtissière in centre of
each round of pastry; top with
an apricot half (see page 122).
Brush pastry with a little egg.
5 Bake pastries about 20 minutes
or until browned lightly. Brush
warm pastries with jam.

crème pâtissière Bring milk,
sugar and extract to the boil
in small saucepan. Meanwhile,
blend cornflour and egg yolks
in medium heatproof bowl;
gradually whisk in hot milk
mixture. Return mixture to pan;
stir over medium heat until
mixture boils and thickens.
Cover surface of custard with
plastic wrap; refrigerate 2 hours.

prep + cook time
1 hour 30 minutes (+ refrigeration)
makes 18
tip You might have a few apricot
halves left over; you only need
18 apricot halves for this recipe.

WALNUT & HONEY TARTS

1 cup (100g) roasted walnuts, chopped coarsely
1 tablespoon cornflour (cornstarch)
½ cup (110g) firmly packed dark brown sugar
2 tablespoons honey
30g (1 ounce) unsalted butter, melted
2 eggs
2 tablespoons thickened (heavy) cream

pastry
1¾ cups (260g) plain (all-purpose) flour
¼ cup (40g) icing (confectioners') sugar
185g (6 ounces) cold unsalted butter, chopped coarsely
1 egg yolk
2 teaspoons iced water, approximately

espresso cream
1 cup (250ml) thickened (heavy) cream
1 tablespoon icing (confectioners') sugar
1 tablespoon cold espresso coffee

1 Make pastry.
2 Grease two 12-hole (2-tablespoon/40ml) deep flat-based patty pans. Cut 24 x 7.5cm (3-inch) rounds from pastry; press rounds into pan holes. Prick bases of cases well with a fork. Refrigerate 30 minutes.
3 Preheat oven to 200°C/400°F.
4 Bake pastry cases about 12 minutes. Cool 30 minutes.
5 Reduce oven to 160°C/325°F.
6 Combine nuts and cornflour in medium bowl; stir in sugar, honey, butter, eggs and cream. Divide filling into cases.
7 Bake tarts about 25 minutes; cool. Refrigerate 30 minutes.
8 Meanwhile, make espresso cream.
9 Serve tarts with espresso cream.

pastry Process flour, sugar and butter until crumbly. With motor operating, add egg yolk and enough of the water to make ingredients come together. Turn dough onto floured surface; knead gently until smooth. Roll half the pastry between sheets of baking paper until 3mm (⅛-inch) thick. Repeat with remaining pastry. Place on trays; refrigerate 30 minutes.

espresso cream Beat ingredients in small bowl with electric mixer until soft peaks form.

prep + cook time
1 hour (+ refrigeration)
makes 24
tip Make sure the tart cases are cool before putting the filling in, otherwise, the filling mixture will seep into the warm pastry and make it soggy.

JAM TARTS

1¾ cups (260g) plain
  (all-purpose) flour
¼ cup (40g) icing
  (confectioners') sugar
185g (6 ounces) cold unsalted
  butter, chopped coarsely
1 egg yolk
2 teaspoons iced water,
  approximately
2 tablespoons each strawberry,
  apricot, raspberry and
  black cherry jams
2 teaspoons icing
  (confectioners') sugar, extra

1 Process flour, sugar and butter until crumbly. With motor operating, add egg yolk and enough of the water to make ingredients come together. Turn dough onto floured surface; knead gently until smooth. Roll half the pastry between sheets of baking paper until 3mm (⅛-inch) thick. Repeat with remaining pastry. Place on trays; refrigerate 30 minutes.
2 Grease two 12-hole (1-tablespoon/20ml) mini muffin pans. Cut 24 x 5.5cm (2¼-inch) rounds from pastry; press rounds into pan holes. Prick bases of cases well with a fork. Refrigerate 30 minutes.
3 Re-roll scraps of pastry between sheets of baking paper until 3mm (⅛-inch) thick. Refrigerate 30 minutes.

4 Preheat oven to 220°C/425°F.
5 Bake pastry cases about 8 minutes. Divide strawberry jam into six cases; repeat with remaining jams and cases. Cut 12 x 3.5cm (1½-inch) rounds from remaining pastry; cut rounds in half. Top tarts with pastry halves.
6 Bake tarts about 10 minutes; cool. Refrigerate 30 minutes. Serve tarts dusted with sifted extra icing sugar.

prep + cook time
45 minutes (+ refrigeration)
makes 24

PLUM & ALMOND TURNOVERS

825g (1¾ pounds) canned whole
    plums in natural juice
¼ cup (55g) caster (superfine)
    sugar
3 cardamom pods, bruised
2 tablespoons cornflour
    (cornstarch)
1 tablespoon water
250g (8 ounces) marzipan,
    chopped coarsely
⅓ cup (80ml) thickened
    (heavy) cream
6 sheets puff pastry
1 egg, beaten lightly
¼ cup (20g) flaked almonds
1 tablespoon demerara sugar

1 Drain plums over small bowl;
reserve ½ cup of juice, discard
remaining. Cut plums into
quarters; discard seeds.
2 Place plums, reserved juice,
caster sugar and cardamom
in medium saucepan; stir over
heat, without boiling, until sugar
dissolves. Bring to the boil; boil,
uncovered, about 5 minutes or
until thickened slightly. Blend
cornflour with the water in small
jug, add to pan; cook, stirring,
until mixture boils and thickens.
Cool 2 hours. Discard cardamom.
3 Meanwhile, blend or process
marzipan and cream until smooth.
4 Preheat oven to 200°C/400°F.
Grease oven trays; line with
baking paper.
5 Cut 30 x 9cm (3¾-inch) rounds
from pastry sheets. Spread
rounded teaspoons of marzipan
mixture over each pastry round,
leaving 1cm (½-inch) border.
Divide plum mixture into centres
of pastry rounds. Brush edges
with egg; fold rounds in half to
enclose filling, pinch edges to
seal. Place on trays, about 5cm
(2 inches) apart.

6 Brush turnovers with egg;
sprinkle with nuts, then demerara
sugar. Use a small sharp knife to
cut two small slits in the top of
each turnover.
7 Bake turnovers about
25 minutes. Cool on trays. Serve
warm, dusted with a little sifted
icing (confectioners') sugar.

prep + cook time
1 hour 10 minutes (+ cooling)
makes 30
serving suggestion Serve warm
with crème anglaise (custard),
cream or ice-cream.

MASCARPONE MATCHSTICKS

½ sheet butter puff pastry,
  thawed
¼ cup (40g) icing
  (confectioners') sugar
200g (6½ ounces) mascarpone
  cheese
½ cup (125ml) thickened
  (heavy) cream
⅓ cup (110g) raspberry jam

1 Preheat oven to 220°C/425°F.
Line oven tray with baking paper.
2 Cut pastry sheet into four
rectangles. Place on oven tray.
Dust pastry with 2 teaspoons of
the sifted icing sugar.
3 Bake pastry about 10 minutes.
Cool. Using serrated knife,
carefully split each rectangle
horizontally.
4 Beat mascarpone, cream and
2 tablespoons of the remaining
sifted icing sugar in small bowl
with electric mixer until soft
peaks form.
5 Spread jam and mascarpone
mixture between pastry pieces.
Serve matchsticks dusted with
remaining sifted icing sugar.

prep + cook time 15 minutes
makes 4

RHUBARB ORANGE PIES

1¾ cups (260g) plain (all-purpose) flour

⅓ cup (55g) icing (confectioners') sugar

185g (6 ounces) cold unsalted butter, chopped coarsely

1 egg yolk

2 teaspoons iced water, approximately

1¼ cups (310ml) thickened (heavy) cream, whipped

1 tablespoon icing (confectioners') sugar, extra

rhubarb orange compote

6 large stalks trimmed rhubarb (375g), chopped coarsely

2 medium oranges (480g), segmented

¼ cup (55g) caster (superfine) sugar

2 teaspoons finely grated orange rind

1 Make rhubarb orange compote.

2 To make shortcrust pastry; process flour, icing sugar and butter until crumbly. With motor operating, add egg yolk and enough of the water to make ingredients come together. Turn dough onto floured surface; knead gently until smooth. Roll half the pastry between sheets of baking paper until 3mm (⅛-inch) thick. Repeat with remaining pastry. Place pastry on trays; refrigerate 30 minutes.

3 Grease two 12-hole (1½-tablespoon/30ml) shallow round-based patty pans.

4 Cut 24 x 6.5cm (2¾-inch) rounds from pastry; press rounds into pan holes, prick well with a fork. Cut 24 x 4.5cm (1¾-inch) rounds from pastry scraps; place on greased oven tray. Refrigerate cases and rounds 30 minutes.

5 Preheat oven to 220°C/425°F.

6 Bake pastry cases and pastry rounds about 12 minutes. Stand cases in pans 10 minutes before transferring to wire rack to cool.

7 Divide compote into cases, top with cream, then pastry rounds. Dust with sifted extra icing sugar.

rhubarb orange compote
Preheat oven to 200°C/400°F. Combine rhubarb and orange in medium baking dish; sprinkle with sugar and rind. Cover dish with foil. Bake about 40 minutes, turning once, until rhubarb is tender. Cool 1 hour. Drain rhubarb mixture; reserve syrup for another use.

prep + cook time
2 hours (+ refrigeration)
makes 24
tips It is fine to use just 300ml carton of cream for this recipe. To segment an orange, use a small sharp knife to slice off the skin and pith using the natural curve of the fruit as a guide. Hold the orange firmly in your hand and gently slide the knife blade between the membrane walls towards the centre of the fruit to release the segments.

There is more art than people imagine in laying a cloth properly... A well laid table is one of the refining influences that home should bear upon the young mind.

– Mrs Beeton's Every Day Cookery, 1893*

Macaroons &
MERINGUES

TROPICAL FRENCH MACAROONS

1 cup (120g) ground almonds
⅓ cup (55g) coarsely chopped
    dried mango
3 egg whites
2 tablespoons caster
    (superfine) sugar
orange food colouring
1¼ cups (240g) pure icing
    (confectioners') sugar
coconut lime filling
⅓ cup (80ml) pouring cream
180g (5½ ounces) white eating
    chocolate, chopped finely
1 teaspoon finely grated
    lime rind
¼ teaspoon coconut extract

1 Grease oven trays; line with baking paper.
2 Process ground almonds and mango until fine.
3 Beat egg whites in small bowl with electric mixer until soft peaks form. Add caster sugar and a little food colouring, beat until sugar dissolves; transfer mixture to large bowl. Fold in sifted icing sugar and almond mixture, in two batches.
4 Spoon mixture into piping bag fitted with 1cm (½-inch) plain tube. Pipe 4cm (1½-inch) rounds, about 2.5cm (1 inch) apart, on trays (see page 123). Tap trays on bench so macaroons spread slightly (see page 123); stand about 30 minutes or until macaroons feel dry to touch.
5 Preheat oven to 150°C/300°F.
6 Bake macaroons about 20 minutes. Cool on trays.
7 Meanwhile, make coconut lime filling.
8 Sandwich macaroons with coconut lime filling.

coconut lime filling Bring cream to the boil in small saucepan. Remove from heat; add chocolate, stir until smooth. Stir in rind and extract. Stand at room temperature until spreadable.

prep + cook time
1 hour (+ standing)
makes 16

BLACK FOREST FRENCH MACAROONS

1¼ cups (100g) desiccated
   coconut
1 tablespoon coarsely chopped
   red glacé cherries
3 egg whites
2 tablespoons caster
   (superfine) sugar
red food colouring
1¼ cups (240g) pure icing
   (confectioners') sugar
2 tablespoons cocoa powder
chocolate cherry filling
⅓ cup (80ml) pouring cream
180g (5½ ounces) dark eating
   (semi-sweet) chocolate,
   chopped finely
1 teaspoon cherry-flavoured
   liqueur

1 Grease oven trays; line with baking paper.
2 Process coconut and cherries until fine.
3 Beat egg whites in small bowl with electric mixer until soft peaks form. Add caster sugar and a little food colouring, beat until sugar dissolves; transfer mixture to large bowl. Fold in sifted icing sugar and cocoa powder and coconut mixture, in two batches.
4 Spoon mixture into piping bag fitted with 1cm (½-inch) plain tube. Pipe 4cm (1½-inch) rounds, about 2.5cm (1-inch) apart, on trays (see page 123). Tap trays on bench so macaroons spread slightly (see page 123); stand about 30 minutes or until macaroons feel dry to touch.

5 Preheat oven to 150°C/300°F.
6 Bake macaroons about 20 minutes. Cool on trays.
7 Meanwhile, make chocolate cherry filling.
8 Sandwich macaroons with chocolate cherry filling.

chocolate cherry filling Bring cream to the boil in small saucepan. Remove from heat; add chocolate, stir until smooth. Stir in liqueur. Stand at room temperature until spreadable.

prep + cook time
1 hour (+ standing)
makes 16

CAPPUCCINO FRENCH MACAROONS

1¼ cups (240g) pure icing
(confectioners') sugar
¾ cup (75g) ground hazelnuts
2 teaspoons instant coffee
granules
1 teaspoon boiling water
3 egg whites
2 tablespoons caster
(superfine) sugar
2 teaspoons cocoa powder
white chocolate ganache
⅓ cup (80ml) pouring cream
180g (5½ ounces) white eating
chocolate, chopped finely

1 Grease oven trays; line with
baking paper.
2 Blend or process icing sugar
and ground hazelnuts until fine.
Sift mixture; discard any coarse
pieces in sifter.
3 Combine coffee and the
boiling water in small bowl.
4 Beat egg whites in small
bowl with electric mixer until
soft peaks form. Add caster
sugar, beat until sugar dissolves;
transfer mixture to large bowl.
Fold in sifted icing sugar, ground
hazelnuts and coffee mixture,
in two batches.
5 Spoon mixture into piping
bag fitted with 1cm (½-inch)
plain tube. Pipe 4cm (1½-inch)
rounds, about 2.5cm (1 inch)
apart, on trays (see page 123).
Tap trays on bench so macaroons
spread slightly (see page 123);
stand about 30 minutes or until
macaroons feel dry to touch.

6 Preheat oven to 150°C/300°F.
7 Bake macaroons about
20 minutes. Cool on trays.
8 Meanwhile, make white
chocolate ganache.
9 Sandwich macaroons with
ganache. Serve dusted with
sifted cocoa powder.

white chocolate ganache
Bring cream to the boil in small
saucepan. Remove from heat;
add chocolate, stir until smooth.
Stand at room temperature until
spreadable.

prep + cook time
1 hour (+ standing)
makes 16

PEPPERMINT FRENCH MACAROONS

1¼ cups (240g) pure icing (confectioners') sugar
1 cup (120g) ground almonds
3 egg whites
2 tablespoons caster (superfine) sugar
green food colouring
1 teaspoon peppermint extract
35g (1 ounces) peppermint crisp, chopped finely
dark chocolate filling
⅓ cup (80ml) pouring cream
180g (5½ ounces) dark eating (semi-sweet) chocolate, chopped finely

1 Grease oven trays; line with baking paper.
2 Blend or process icing sugar and ground almonds until fine. Sift mixture; discard any coarse pieces in sifter.
3 Beat egg whites in small bowl with electric mixer until soft peaks form. Add caster sugar and a little food colouring, beat until sugar dissolves; transfer mixture to large bowl. Fold in sifted icing sugar, ground almonds and extract, in two batches.
4 Spoon mixture into piping bag fitted with 1cm (½-inch) plain tube. Pipe 4cm (1½-inch) rounds, about 2.5cm (1 inch) apart, on trays (see page 123). Tap trays on bench so macaroons spread slightly (see page 123); stand about 30 minutes or until macaroons feel dry to touch.

5 Preheat oven to 150°C/300°F.
6 Bake macaroons about 20 minutes. Cool on trays.
7 Meanwhile, make dark chocolate filling.
8 Spread macaroons with filling. Sprinkle half the macaroons with peppermint crisp; top with remaining macaroons.
dark chocolate filling Bring cream to the boil in small saucepan. Remove from heat; add chocolate, stir until smooth. Stand at room temperature until spreadable.

prep + cook time
1 hour (+ standing)
makes 16

RASPBERRY MERINGUES
WITH ROSEWATER CREAM

250g (8 ounces) fresh raspberries
3 egg whites
¾ cup (165g) caster (superfine) sugar
1¼ cups (310ml) thickened (heavy) cream
1 tablespoon icing (confectioners') sugar
1 teaspoon rosewater

1 Preheat oven to 120°C/250°F. Grease two oven trays, line with baking paper.

2 Push 80g (2½ ounces) of the raspberries through fine sieve into small bowl; discard seeds. Cut remaining raspberries in half.

3 Beat egg whites in small bowl with electric mixer until soft peaks form. Gradually add caster sugar, one tablespoon at a time, beating until sugar dissolves between additions. Fold in raspberry puree for marbled effect.

4 Using large metal spoon, spoon meringue into 12 freeform shapes on trays (see page 123).

5 Bake meringues about 1½ hours. Cool meringues in oven with door ajar.

6 Meanwhile, beat cream, icing sugar and rosewater in small bowl with electric mixer until soft peaks form.

7 Top meringues with cream and raspberry halves.

prep + cook time
1 hour 50 minutes (+ cooling)
makes 12
tip It is fine to use just one 300ml carton of cream for this recipe.

PASSIONFRUIT MERINGUE CUPCAKES

125g (4 ounces) unsalted butter, softened
2 teaspoons finely grated lemon rind
⅔ cup (150g) caster (superfine) sugar
2 eggs
1¼ cups (185g) self-raising flour
⅓ cup (80ml) milk
passionfruit curd
4 egg yolks
⅓ cup (75g) caster (superfine) sugar
⅓ cup (80ml) passionfruit pulp
50g (1½ ounces) unsalted butter, chopped coarsely
passionfruit meringue
3 egg whites
¾ cup (165g) caster (superfine) sugar
1 tablespoon passionfruit pulp
yellow food colouring

1 Make passionfruit curd.
2 Preheat oven to 180°C/350°F. Line 20 holes of two 12-hole (2-tablespoon/40ml) deep flat-based patty pans with paper cases.
3 Beat butter, rind, sugar and eggs in small bowl with electric mixer until light and fluffy. Stir in sifted flour and milk, in two batches. Divide mixture into paper cases.
4 Bake cakes about 20 minutes. Stand cakes in pan 5 minutes before turning, top-side up, onto wire racks to cool. Increase oven to 240°C/475°F.
5 Make passionfruit meringue.
6 Cut a 1cm (½-inch) deep hole in centre of each cake, discard cake tops; fill holes with curd. Place cakes on oven trays.
7 Drop heaped tablespoons of meringue on top of each cake. Bake about 5 minutes or until meringue is browned lightly.

passionfruit curd Stir ingredients in small heatproof bowl over small saucepan of simmering water about 10 minutes or until mixture coats the back of a spoon. Cover surface of curd with plastic wrap; refrigerate overnight.
passionfruit meringue Beat egg whites in small bowl with electric mixer until soft peaks form. Gradually add sugar, one tablespoon at a time, beating until sugar dissolves between additions. Fold in passionfruit and a little colouring.

prep + cook time
1 hour 10 minutes
(+ refrigeration & cooling)
makes 20

MARSHMALLOW CUPCAKES

150g (4½ ounces) unsalted
  butter, softened
½ teaspoon vanilla extract
⅔ cup (150g) caster
  (superfine) sugar
2 eggs
⅓ cup (50g) self-raising flour
½ cup (75g) plain (all-purpose)
  flour
½ cup (60g) ground almonds
⅓ cup (110g) strawberry jam
1 tablespoon desiccated
  coconut
marshmallow frosting
2 eggs whites
1 cup (220g) caster
  (superfine) sugar
¼ cup (60ml) cold water
1 tablespoon glucose syrup
1 teaspoon rosewater
pink food colouring

1 Preheat oven to 180°C/350°F. Line 12-hole (⅓-cup/80ml) muffin pan with paper cases.
2 Beat butter, extract, sugar and eggs in small bowl with electric mixer until light and fluffy. Stir in sifted flours and ground almonds, in two batches. Divide mixture into paper cases.
3 Bake cakes about 25 minutes. Stand cakes in pan 5 minutes before turning, top-side up, onto wire rack to cool.
4 Meanwhile, make marshmallow frosting.
5 Cut a 2cm (¾-inch) deep hole in centre of each cake, fill with jam; replace cake tops.
6 Spoon marshmallow frosting into piping bag fitted with 2cm (¾-inch) fluted tube. Pipe frosting on top of each cake; sprinkle with coconut.

marshmallow frosting Combine egg whites, sugar, the water and glucose syrup in medium bowl; over medium saucepan of simmering water. Beat mixture using hand-held beater, on low speed, 3 minutes. Increase speed to high; beat about 4 minutes or until soft peaks form. Remove from heat. Add rosewater and a little food colouring; beat, on high speed, about 2 minutes or until frosting is thick.

prep + cook time
1 hour 10 minutes (+ cooling)
makes 12
tip Make the marshmallow frosting when you are ready to pipe it onto the cakes; it becomes hard to work with after standing.

LEMON MERINGUE PIE

½ cup (75g) cornflour
(cornstarch)
1 cup (220g) caster (superfine)
sugar
½ cup (125ml) lemon juice
1¼ cups (310ml) water
2 teaspoons finely grated
lemon rind
60g (2 ounces) unsalted butter,
chopped coarsely
3 eggs, separated
½ cup (110g) caster (superfine)
sugar, extra

pastry
1½ cups (225g) plain
(all-purpose) flour
1 tablespoon icing
(confectioners') sugar
140g (4½ ounces) cold butter,
chopped coarsely
1 egg yolk
2 tablespoons cold water

1 Make pastry.
2 Grease 24cm (9½-inch) round loose-based fluted flan pan. Roll pastry between sheets of baking paper until large enough to line pan. Ease pastry into pan, press into base and side; trim edge. Cover; refrigerate 30 minutes.
3 Preheat oven to 200°C/400°F.
4 Place pan on oven tray. Line pastry case with baking paper; fill with dried beans or rice. Bake 15 minutes; remove paper and beans carefully from pastry case. Bake about 10 minutes; cool pastry case, turn oven off.
5 Meanwhile, combine cornflour and sugar in medium saucepan; gradually stir in juice and the water until smooth. Cook, stirring, over high heat, until mixture boils and thickens. Reduce heat; simmer, stirring, 1 minute. Remove from heat; stir in rind, butter and egg yolks. Cool 10 minutes.
6 Spread filling into pastry case (see page 123). Cover; refrigerate 2 hours.

7 Preheat oven to 220°C/425°F.
8 Beat egg whites in small bowl with electric mixer until soft peaks form; gradually add extra sugar, beating until sugar dissolves.
9 Roughen surface of filling with fork before spreading with meringue mixture (see page 123). Bake about 2 minutes or until meringue is browned lightly.

pastry Process flour, icing sugar and butter until crumbly. Add egg yolk and the water; process until ingredients come together. Knead dough on floured surface until smooth. Wrap pastry in plastic; refrigerate 30 minutes.

prep + cook time
1 hour 10 minutes (+ refrigeration)
serves 10

SNOW EGGS WITH BLACKBERRY FOOL

35g (1 ounce) unsalted butter

2 tablespoons light brown sugar

1½ tablespoons golden syrup
  or treacle

¼ cup (35g) plain (all-purpose)
  flour

½ teaspoon lemon juice

4 egg whites

1 cup (160g) icing
  (confectioners') sugar

2 tablespoons icing
  (confectioners') sugar, extra

blackberry fool

300g (9½ ounces) blackberries

1 cup (250ml) thickened
  (heavy) cream

1 cup (230g) thick vanilla custard

1 Preheat oven to 180°C/350°F.

2 Grease three oven trays. Trace eight 11cm (4¼-inch) rounds, about 5cm (2 inches) apart, onto three sheets baking paper to use as a guide; line trays with paper, marked-side down.

3 To make snaps, stir butter, brown sugar and golden syrup in small saucepan, over low heat, until smooth. Remove from heat; stir in sifted flour and juice. Using a wet, thin metal spatula, spread mixture into marked rounds on trays.

4 Bake snaps about 12 minutes or until they bubble and are golden brown. Slide a thin metal spatula under each snap to loosen; working quickly, shape one snap over back of silicone egg poacher mould (see page 122). Transfer to wire rack to cool. Repeat with remaining snaps.

5 To make snow eggs, half fill a large frying pan with water; bring to the boil. Reduce heat to gentle simmer. Meanwhile, beat egg whites in small bowl with electric mixer until soft peaks form. Gradually add icing sugar, about one tablespoon at a time; beat about 5 minutes, or until mixture is thick. Spoon ½ cup of the meringue mixture into greased silicone egg poacher moulds; smooth surface. Place moulds in simmering water about 5 minutes or until meringue is firm (see page 122). Using slotted spoon carefully remove moulds from pan; stand 1 minute. Transfer snow eggs onto baking-paper-lined tray; gently turn moulds inside out to release the snow eggs (see page 122). Repeat with remaining meringue mixture.

6 Make blackberry fool.

7 Divide blackberry fool into serving glasses; top with snow eggs and snaps. Dust with sifted extra icing sugar.

blackberry fool Roughly mash blackberries in small bowl with fork. Beat cream in small bowl with electric mixer until soft peaks form; fold in custard, then blackberries for marbled effect.

prep + cook time

1 hour 20 minutes **serves** 8

tips If using frozen blackberries, ensure they are thawed and drained well on absorbent paper, before mashing with fork. We used two (½-cup/125ml) silicone egg poacher moulds at a time, for this recipe – they are available in specialty kitchenware and chef supply stores.

WHITE CHOCOLATE & PASSIONFRUIT MARSHMALLOW BISCUITS

60g (2 ounces) unsalted butter, softened
¼ cup (55g) caster (superfine) sugar
1 egg
½ teaspoon vanilla extract
1 cup (150g) plain (all-purpose) flour
2 tablespoons custard powder
180g (5½ ounces) white eating chocolate, melted

passionfruit marshmallow
¼ cup (60ml) passionfruit pulp
¾ cup (165g) caster (superfine) sugar
⅓ cup (80ml) hot water
3 teaspoons gelatine
2 tablespoons cold water
yellow food colouring

1 Make passionfruit marshmallow.
2 Meanwhile, beat butter, sugar, egg and extract in small bowl with electric mixer until combined. Stir in sifted flour and custard powder. Roll dough between sheets of baking paper until 5mm (¼-inch) thick; place on tray. Refrigerate 30 minutes.
3 Preheat oven to 180°C/350°F. Line oven trays with baking paper.
4 Cut 24 x 5.5cm (2½-inch) rounds from dough. Place rounds, about 2.5cm (1 inch) apart, on trays.
5 Bake biscuits about 12 minutes. Cool on trays.
6 Working quickly, spread ½ teaspoon of the melted chocolate onto centre of each biscuit; immediately top with marshmallow, flat-side down (see page 123). Place biscuits on wire rack over baking-paper-lined tray; pipe or drizzle with remaining chocolate (see page 123). Stand at room temperature until set.

passionfruit marshmallow
Grease two 12-hole (1½-tablespoon/30ml) shallow round-based patty pans. Stir passionfruit, sugar and the hot water in small saucepan, over low heat, until sugar dissolves. Combine gelatine and the cold water in small jug. Pour gelatine mixture into hot sugar syrup; cook, stirring, until gelatine dissolves. Pour mixture into small heatproof bowl; cool to room temperature. Beat mixture and a little food colouring with electric mixer, on high speed, about 8 minutes or until mixture is thick and holds its shape. Working quickly, spoon the mixture into pan holes; smooth surfaces. Stand at room temperature about 1 hour or until firm. Slide marshmallows out of pan holes.

prep + cook time
50 minutes (+ standing)
makes 24

CHOC MALT MERINGUES

3 egg whites
½ cup (110g) firmly packed
   light brown sugar
⅔ cup (110g) icing
   (confectioners') sugar
¼ cup (25g) cocoa powder
2 tablespoons malted
   milk powder
150g (4½ ounces) milk eating
   chocolate, melted

1 Preheat oven to 120°C/250°F. Grease three oven trays. Trace 22 x 6cm (2½-inch) rounds, in total, about 2.5cm (1-inch) apart, onto three sheets baking paper to use as a guide; line trays with paper, marked-side down.

2 Beat egg whites in small bowl with electric mixer until soft peaks form. Add brown sugar, beat until sugar dissolves. Fold in sifted icing sugar, cocoa and malt powder.

3 Spoon mixture into piping bag fitted with 1cm (½-inch) plain tube. Pipe mixture into rounds on trays, using paper as a guide (see page 123).

4 Bake meringues about 2 hours. Cool in oven with door ajar.

5 Dip tops of meringues in melted chocolate. Stand at room temperature until set. Dust with a little extra sifted icing sugar.

prep + cook time
2 hours 20 minutes (+ standing)
makes 22

Cakes
LARGE & SMALL

CREAMY COCONUT CAKE

250g (8 ounces) unsalted butter, softened
1½ cups (330g) caster (superfine) sugar
½ cup (125ml) coconut cream
4 eggs, separated
1½ cups (225g) plain (all-purpose) flour
1 cup (150g) self-raising flour
1 cup (250ml) buttermilk
2 cups (100g) flaked coconut

coconut frosting
375g (12 ounces) cream cheese, softened
100g (3 ounces) unsalted butter, softened
2 teaspoons coconut extract
2 cups (320g) icing (confectioners') sugar
⅓ cup (80ml) coconut cream
1 cup (80g) desiccated coconut

1 Preheat oven to 170°C/340°F. Grease two deep 22cm (9-inch) round cake pans.
2 Beat butter, sugar and coconut cream in small bowl with electric mixer until light and fluffy. Beat in eggs yolks until combined. Transfer mixture to large bowl; stir in sifted flours and buttermilk, in two batches.
3 Beat egg whites in small bowl with electric mixer until soft peaks form. Fold egg whites into cake mixture, in two batches. Divide mixture between pans.
4 Bake cakes about 50 minutes. Stand cakes in pan 10 minutes before turning, top-side up, onto wire rack to cool.
5 Meanwhile, make coconut frosting.
6 Split cakes in half. Place one layer on serving plate, cut-side up; spread with ⅔ cup of frosting. Repeat layering, finishing with remaining frosting spread over top and side of cake. Press flaked coconut all over cake.

coconut frosting Beat cream cheese, butter and extract in large bowl until smooth. Beat in sifted icing sugar and coconut cream, in three batches; stir in coconut.

prep + cook time
2 hours (+ cooling)
serves 16
tip We bought flaked coconut from a store which stocks Indian and Fijian food. If you want to make your own flaked coconut as seen on the cover of this book, buy a small brown-husked coconut (700g). Preheat oven to 220°C/425°F. Pierce eyes of the coconut, drain and discard liquid. Place coconut on oven tray; bake about 10 minutes or until cracks appear. Carefully split the coconut open by hitting with a hammer; remove flesh. Using vegetable peeler, slice coconut flesh into curls.

MINI BOSTON CREAM CAKES

3 eggs
½ cup (110g) caster (superfine) sugar
¾ cup (110g) self-raising flour
20g (¾ ounce) unsalted butter
¼ cup (60ml) boiling water
185g (6 ounces) dark eating (semi-sweet) chocolate, chopped coarsely
60g (2 ounces) unsalted butter, extra
crème pâtissière
1 vanilla bean
1 cup (250ml) milk
⅓ cup (75g) caster (superfine) sugar
2 tablespoons cornflour (cornstarch)
3 egg yolks
⅓ cup (80ml) thick (double) cream

1 Make crème pâtissière.
2 Preheat oven to 180°C/350°F. Grease 12-hole (½-cup/125ml) oval friand pan with butter; dust lightly with a little extra flour.
3 Beat eggs and sugar in small bowl with electric mixer about 5 minutes or until thick and creamy. Transfer mixture to large bowl; fold in sifted flour, then combined butter and the boiling water. Divide mixture into pan holes.
4 Bake cakes about 15 minutes. Working quickly, use a small knife to loosen edges of cakes from pan; turn immediately onto baking-paper-covered wire rack to cool.
5 Stir chocolate and extra butter in small heatproof bowl over small saucepan of simmering water until smooth.
6 Split cold cakes in half, sandwich with crème pâtissière. Top with chocolate mixture.

crème pâtissière Split vanilla bean lengthways; scrape seeds into small saucepan, discard bean. Add milk and sugar to pan; bring to the boil. Meanwhile, combine cornflour and egg yolks in medium heatproof bowl; gradually whisk in hot milk mixture. Return custard to pan; stir over heat until mixture boils and thickens. Cover surface of custard with plastic wrap; cool to room temperature. Fold cream into custard.

prep + cook time
1 hour 10 minutes (+ cooling)
makes 12

CHOC-MALT CUPCAKES

185g (6 ounces) unsalted butter,
   softened
¾ cup (165g) caster
   (superfine) sugar
3 eggs
1 cup (150g) self-raising flour
½ cup (75g) plain (all-purpose)
   flour
2 tablespoons cocoa powder
2 tablespoons malted
   milk powder
½ cup (125ml) milk
1 cup (125g) choc-coated malt
   balls, chopped coarsely
malted milk frosting
125g (4 ounces) unsalted butter,
   softened
⅓ cup (40g) malted milk powder
2 cups (320g) icing
   (confectioners') sugar
¼ cup (60ml) pouring cream

1 Preheat oven to 180°C/350°F.
Line 15 holes of two 12-hole
(⅓-cup/80ml) muffin pans with
paper cases.
2 Beat butter, sugar, eggs,
sifted flours, powders and milk in
medium bowl with electric mixer
on low speed until ingredients
are combined. Increase speed
to medium; beat until mixture
is changed to a paler colour.
Divide mixture into paper cases;
smooth surface.
3 Bake cakes about 25 minutes.
Stand cakes in pan 10 minutes
before turning, top-side up, onto
wire rack to cool.
4 Meanwhile, make malted
milk frosting.
5 Spread cakes with frosting;
sprinkle with malt balls.

malted milk frosting Beat
butter and malted milk powder
in small bowl with electric mixer
until light and fluffy. Beat in
sifted icing sugar and cream,
in two batches.

prep + cook time 55 minutes
makes 15

RASPBERRY TRIFLE CUPCAKES

90g (3 ounces) unsalted butter, softened
½ teaspoon vanilla extract
½ cup (110g) caster (superfine) sugar
2 eggs
1 cup (150g) self-raising flour
2 tablespoons milk
⅔ cup (100g) frozen raspberries
2 tablespoons sweet sherry
125g (4 ounces) fresh raspberries
whipped custard icing
2 tablespoons custard powder
2 tablespoons caster (superfine) sugar
1 cup (250ml) pouring cream
1 cup (250ml) thickened (heavy) cream

1 Make whipped custard icing.
2 Meanwhile, preheat oven to 180°C/350°F. Line 12-hole (⅓-cup/80ml) muffin pan with paper cases.
3 Beat butter, extract, sugar, eggs, sifted flour and milk in small bowl with electric mixer on low speed until ingredients are combined. Increase speed to medium; beat until mixture is changed to a paler colour. Fold in frozen raspberries. Divide mixture into paper cases; smooth surface.
4 Bake cakes about 30 minutes. Stand cakes in pan 10 minutes before turning, top-side up, onto wire rack to cool. Brush warm cakes with sherry.
5 Top cakes with icing and fresh raspberries. Dust with a little extra sifted icing sugar.

whipped custard icing Blend custard powder and sugar with pouring cream in small saucepan; stir over heat until mixture boils and thickens. Remove from heat. Cover surface of custard with plastic wrap; cool 20 minutes. Refrigerate 1 hour. Beat cold custard in small bowl with electric mixer until smooth. Add thickened cream; beat until soft peaks form.

prep + cook time
1 hour 10 minutes
(+ cooling & refrigeration)
makes 12

PINK & BROWN CUPCAKES

60g (2 ounces) dark eating (semi-sweet) chocolate, chopped coarsely
⅔ cup (160ml) milk
90g (3 ounces) unsalted butter, softened
1 cup (220g) firmly packed light brown sugar
2 eggs
⅔ cup (100g) self-raising flour
2 tablespoons cocoa powder
⅓ cup (40g) ground almonds
⅔ cup (100g) frozen raspberries
meringue butter cream
3 eggs whites
¾ cup (165g) caster (superfine) sugar
225g (7 ounces) unsalted butter, softened
1½ teaspoons vanilla extract
pink food colouring

1 Preheat oven to 180°C/350°F. Line 30 holes from three 12-hole (2-tablespoon/40ml) deep flat-based patty pans with paper cases.

2 Stir chocolate and milk in small saucepan over low heat until smooth.

3 Beat butter, sugar and eggs in small bowl with electric mixer until combined. Transfer mixture to large bowl. Stir in sifted flour and cocoa, ground almonds, then warm chocolate mixture; fold in raspberries. Divide mixture into paper cases.

4 Bake cakes about 25 minutes. Stand cakes in pan 10 minutes before turning, top-side up, onto wire rack to cool.

5 Meanwhile, make meringue butter cream.

6 Spoon meringue butter cream into piping bag fitted with 2cm (¾-inch) fluted tube. Pipe meringue butter cream onto cakes.

meringue butter cream Place egg whites and sugar in medium bowl over a medium saucepan of simmering water; beat with hand-held beater about 3 minutes or until sugar is dissolved. Remove from heat; beat, on high speed, about 10 minutes or until frosting is thick. Beat in butter, in batches, until combined between additions. Beat in extract and few drops food colouring.

prep + cook time
1 hour (+ cooling)
makes 30

PEACHES & CREAM CUPCAKES

90g (3 ounces) unsalted butter,
softened
90g (3 ounces) cream cheese,
softened
⅔ cup (150g) caster
(superfine) sugar
2 eggs
½ cup (75g) plain (all-purpose)
flour
⅓ cup (50g) self-raising flour
2 teaspoons orange
blossom water
¾ cup (120g) finely chopped
dried peaches
⅔ cup (160ml) water
2 tablespoons caster (superfine)
sugar, extra
1¼ cups (310ml) thickened
(heavy) cream
1 tablespoon icing
(confectioners') sugar

1 Preheat oven to 180°C/350°F.
Line 12-hole (⅓-cup/80ml) muffin
pan with paper cases.
2 Beat butter, cream cheese,
caster sugar and eggs in small
bowl with electric mixer until
light and fluffy. Add sifted flours
and orange blossom water; beat
on low speed until combined.
Divide mixture into paper cases;
smooth surface.
3 Bake cakes about 25 minutes.
Stand cakes in pan 10 minutes
before turning, top-side up, onto
wire rack to cool.
4 Meanwhile, combine peaches,
the water and extra caster sugar
in small saucepan; bring to the
boil. Boil, uncovered, about
10 minutes or until peaches
are soft and liquid is almost
absorbed. Cool.

5 Cut a 2cm (¾-inch) deep hole
in centre of each cake; fill with
half the peach mixture. Discard
cake tops.
6 Beat cream and icing sugar
in small bowl with electric mixer
until soft peaks form. Top cakes
with whipped cream and
remaining peach mixture.

prep + cook time
55 minutes (+ cooling)
makes 12
tip It is fine to use just one 300ml
carton of cream for this recipe.

CINNAMON SWIRL CUPCAKES

155g (5 ounces) unsalted butter,
   softened
⅓ cup (75g) firmly packed
   light brown sugar
3 teaspoons ground cinnamon
2 teaspoons cocoa powder
1 cup (220g) caster (superfine)
   sugar
2 eggs
¾ cup (110g) plain (all-purpose)
   flour
1 cup (150g) self-raising flour
½ cup (125ml) buttermilk
2 teaspoons cinnamon sugar
cream cheese frosting
60g (2 ounces) unsalted butter,
   softened
160g (5 ounces) cream cheese,
   softened
3 cups (480g) icing
   (confectioners') sugar

1 Melt 30g (1 ounce) of the butter in small saucepan. Remove from heat; stir in brown sugar, ground cinnamon and cocoa. Cool.

2 Preheat oven to 180°C/350°F. Line 12-hole (⅓-cup/80ml) muffin pans with paper cases.

3 Beat remaining butter, caster sugar, eggs, sifted flours and buttermilk in medium bowl with electric mixer on low speed until ingredients are combined. Increase speed to medium; beat until mixture is changed to a paler colour. Fold in brown sugar mixture, for marbled effect. Divide mixture into paper cases.

4 Bake cakes about 25 minutes. Stand cakes in pan 10 minutes before turning, top-side up, onto wire rack to cool.

5 Meanwhile, make cream cheese frosting.

6 Spread frosting onto cakes; dust with cinnamon sugar.

cream cheese frosting Beat butter and cream cheese in small bowl with electric mixer until light and fluffy; gradually beat in sifted icing sugar.

prep + cook time 55 minutes
makes 12

RASPBERRY POWDER PUFFS

2 eggs
⅓ cup (75g) caster (superfine)
    sugar
2 tablespoons pure cornflour
    (cornstarch)
2 tablespoons plain
    (all-purpose) flour
2 tablespoons self-raising flour
½ cup (125ml) thickened
    (heavy) cream
2 tablespoons icing
    (confectioners') sugar
1 cup (120g) fresh raspberries,
    chopped coarsely

1 Preheat oven to 180°C/350°F. Butter and flour 28 holes from three 12-hole (1½-tablespoon/ 30ml) shallow round-based patty pans.
2 Beat eggs and caster sugar in small bowl with electric mixer about 4 minutes or until thick and creamy.
3 Sift flours twice onto baking paper, then sift a third time over egg mixture; fold flour into egg mixture. Drop level tablespoons of mixture into pan holes.
4 Bake puffs about 12 minutes; immediately turn puffs onto wire racks to cool.

5 Beat cream and half the icing sugar in small bowl with electric mixer until soft peaks form; fold in berries.
6 Sandwich puffs with raspberry cream just before serving. Dust with sifted remaining icing sugar.

prep + cook time 1 hour
makes 14
tip You can use any fresh berries you like in this recipe.

NEAPOLITAN MERINGUE CUPCAKES

125g (4 ounces) unsalted butter, chopped coarsely

80g (2½ ounces) white eating chocolate, chopped coarsely

1 cup (220g) caster (superfine) sugar

½ cup (125ml) milk

½ cup (75g) plain (all-purpose) flour

½ cup (75g) self-raising flour

1 egg

1 cup (250ml) neapolitan ice-cream

meringue

3 egg whites

¾ cup (165g) caster (superfine) sugar

1 Preheat oven to 180°C/350°F. Line 12-hole (⅓-cup/80ml) muffin pan with paper cases.

2 Stir butter, chocolate, sugar and milk in small saucepan over low heat until smooth. Transfer mixture to medium bowl; cool 15 minutes.

3 Whisk in sifted flours, then egg. Divide mixture into cases.

4 Bake cakes about 30 minutes. Stand cakes in pan 10 minutes before turning, top-side up, onto wire rack to cool.

5 Using a sharp pointed knife, cut a deep hole in the centre of each cake; reserve cut out cake. Fill each hole with a level tablespoon of ice-cream, top with reserved cake. Place cakes on oven tray; freeze.

6 Preheat oven to 220°C/425°F.

7 Meanwhile, make meringue.

8 Top cakes with meringue. Bake about 2 minutes or until meringue is browned lightly. Serve immediately.

meringue Beat egg whites and sugar in small bowl with electric mixer until sugar is dissolved.

prep + cook time
1 hour 10 minutes
(+ cooling & freezing)
makes 12

MIXED SPICE & HONEY POWDER PUFFS

2 eggs
⅓ cup (75g) caster (superfine)
   sugar
2 tablespoons pure cornflour
   (cornstarch)
2 tablespoons plain
   (all-purpose) flour
2 tablespoons self-raising flour
1 teaspoon mixed spice
½ cup (125ml) thickened
   (heavy) cream
1 tablespoon honey
2 teaspoons pure icing
   (confectioner's) sugar

1 Preheat oven to 180°C/350°F. Butter and flour 28 holes from three 12-hole (1½-tablespoon/30ml) shallow round-based patty pans.
2 Beat eggs and caster sugar in small bowl with electric mixer about 4 minutes or until thick and creamy.
3 Sift flours and spice twice onto baking paper, then sift a third time over egg mixture; fold flour mixture into egg mixture. Drop level tablespoons of mixture into pan holes.
4 Bake puffs about 12 minutes. Immediately turn puffs onto wire racks to cool.

5 Beat cream and honey in small bowl with electric mixer until soft peaks form.
6 Sandwich puffs with honey cream just before serving. Dust with sifted icing sugar.

prep + cook time 1 hour
makes 14

BROWN SUGAR CARAMEL SPONGE

395g (12½ ounces) canned
    sweetened condensed milk
4 eggs
¾ cup (165g) firmly packed
    dark brown sugar
1 cup (150g) self-raising flour
20g (¾ ounce) unsalted butter
¼ cup (60ml) boiling water
1¼ cups (310ml) thickened
    (heavy) cream, whipped

1 Preheat oven to 240°C/475°F.

2 Pour condensed milk into medium shallow baking dish; cover with foil. Place dish in large baking dish; add enough boiling water to large dish to come halfway up sides of dish. Bake uncovered about 1¼ hours or until condensed milk is golden brown. Cool to room temperature. Whisk caramel until smooth.

3 Reduce oven to 180°C/350°F. Grease two deep 23cm (9-inch) round cake pans.

4 Beat eggs and sugar in small bowl with electric mixer about 10 minutes or until thick and creamy; transfer mixture to large bowl.

5 Sift flour twice onto baking paper, then sift over egg mixture; fold in flour, then combined butter and the boiling water. Divide mixture between pans.

6 Bake sponges about 20 minutes. Turn sponges immediately onto baking-paper-covered wire racks to cool.

7 Place one sponge on serving plate; spread with half the whipped cream, drizzle with half the caramel. Top with remaining sponge, cream and caramel.

prep + cook time
1 hour 55 minutes (+ cooling)
serves 12
tip It is fine to use just one 300ml carton of cream for this recipe.

Strict cleanliness must be observed in pastry-making; all the utensils used should be perfectly free from dust and dirt, and the things required for pastry kept entirely for that purpose.

– MRS BEETON'S EVERY DAY COOKERY, 1893*

WHOOPIE PIES &
Popcakes

CHOC-MINT WHOOPIE PIES

125g (4 ounces) unsalted butter,
  softened
½ cup (110g) firmly packed
  light brown sugar
1 egg
¾ cup (110g) plain (all-purpose)
  flour
¼ cup (35g) self-raising flour
1 teaspoon bicarbonate of soda
  (baking soda)
⅓ cup (35g) cocoa powder
⅔ cup (160ml) buttermilk
mint butter cream
125g (4 ounces) unsalted butter,
  softened
1½ cups (240g) icing
  (confectioners') sugar
1 tablespoon milk
1 teaspoon peppermint extract
green food colouring
chocolate ganache
¼ cup (60ml) pouring cream
100g (3 ounces) dark eating
  (semi-sweet) chocolate,
  chopped finely

1 Preheat oven to 200°C/400°F.
Grease and line oven trays with
baking paper.
2 Beat butter, sugar and egg
in small bowl with electric mixer
until light and fluffy. Beat in sifted
dry ingredients and buttermilk,
in two batches, on low speed,
until mixture is smooth.
3 Drop level tablespoons of
mixture onto trays, about 4cm
(1½ inches) apart.
4 Bake pies about 8 minutes.
Cool on trays.
5 Meanwhile, make mint butter
cream and chocolate ganache.
6 Sandwich whoopie pies with
butter cream and ganache.

mint butter cream Beat butter
in small bowl with electric mixer
until as white as possible. Beat in
sifted icing sugar, then milk and
extract; tint green.
chocolate ganache Bring cream
to the boil in small saucepan.
Remove from heat; add
chocolate, stir until smooth.

prep + cook time 55 minutes
makes 16
tip When you drop the whoopie
pie mixture onto trays ensure
that the mixture is in round shape.
The shape that the mixture is
dropped onto the trays will be
similar to the cooked shape.

RED VELVET WHOOPIE PIES

125g (4 ounces) unsalted butter, softened
½ cup (110g) caster (superfine) sugar
1 egg
¾ cup (110g) plain (all-purpose) flour
⅓ cup (50g) self-raising flour
1 teaspoon bicarbonate of soda (baking soda)
¼ cup (25g) cocoa powder
⅔ cup (160ml) buttermilk
2 teaspoons rose pink food colouring
1 tablespoon tiny silver cachous
cream cheese filling
250g (8 ounces) cream cheese, softened
½ cup (80g) icing (confectioners') sugar
½ teaspoon vanilla extract
⅔ cup (160ml) thickened (heavy) cream

1 Preheat oven to 200°C/400°F. Grease and line oven trays with baking paper.
2 Beat butter, sugar and egg in small bowl with electric mixer until light and fluffy. Beat in sifted dry ingredients, buttermilk and food colouring, in two batches, on low speed, until mixture is smooth.
3 Drop level tablespoons of mixture onto trays, about 4cm (1½ inches) apart.
4 Bake pies about 8 minutes. Cool on trays.
5 Meanwhile, make cream cheese filling.
6 Spoon cream cheese filling into piping bag fitted with 2cm (¾-inch) fluted tube. Pipe filling onto flat side of half the pies; sandwich with remaining pies. Sprinkle edges of filling with cachous. Dust with a little extra sifted icing sugar.

cream cheese filling Beat cream cheese, sifted sugar and extract in small bowl with electric mixer until smooth. Beat in cream.

prep + cook time 55 minutes
makes 16

MINI BROWN SUGAR & HAZELNUT WHOOPIE PIES

125g (4 ounces) unsalted butter, softened

½ cup (110g) firmly packed dark brown sugar

1 egg

⅔ cup (100g) plain (all-purpose) flour

¼ cup (35g) self-raising flour

1 teaspoon bicarbonate of soda (baking soda)

⅔ cup (70g) ground hazelnuts

⅔ cup (160ml) buttermilk

1 tablespoon icing (confectioners') sugar

hazelnut butter cream

160g (5 ounces) unsalted butter, softened

2 cups (320g) icing (confectioners') sugar

2 tablespoons hazelnut-flavoured liqueur

buttered hazelnuts

1 cup (220g) caster (superfine) sugar

⅓ cup (80ml) water

1½ teaspoons glucose syrup

10g (½ ounce) butter

3 teaspoons dark rum

½ cup (70g) hazelnuts

1 Preheat oven to 200°C/400°F. Grease and line oven trays with baking paper.

2 Beat butter, brown sugar and egg in small bowl with electric mixer until light and fluffy. Beat in sifted dry ingredients, ground hazelnuts and buttermilk, in two batches, on low speed, until mixture is smooth.

3 Drop heaped teaspoons of mixture onto trays, about 4cm (1½ inches) apart.

4 Bake pies about 8 minutes. Cool on trays.

5 Meanwhile, make hazelnut butter cream and then buttered hazelnuts.

6 Sandwich pies with two-thirds of the butter cream. Top pies with remaining butter cream; sprinkle with buttered hazelnuts. Dust with sifted icing sugar.

hazelnut butter cream Beat butter in small bowl with electric mixer until as white as possible. Beat in sifted icing sugar, then liqueur.

buttered hazelnuts Stir sugar, the water and glucose in small saucepan over heat, without boiling, until sugar dissolves. Bring to the boil; boil, uncovered, without stirring, until syrup reaches 112°C/235°F on candy thermometer or when a small amount of syrup, dropped into cold water, moulds easily into soft ball using fingertips. Add butter and rum to syrup; boil, uncovered, about 10 minutes or until mixture is golden. Remove from heat, add nuts, do not stir; return to heat 1 minute. Working quickly, lift out nuts, one at a time, with a fork, and place on greased oven tray. Allow to set at room temperature.

prep + cook time
1 hour 10 minutes (+ cooling)
makes 28

LEMON GINGER-SPICE WHOOPIE PIES

125g (4 ounces) unsalted butter, softened

½ cup (110g) firmly packed dark brown sugar

1 egg

1¼ cups (185g) plain (all-purpose) flour

¼ cup (35g) self-raising flour

1 teaspoon bicarbonate of soda (baking soda)

3 teaspoons ground ginger

½ teaspoon each ground cinnamon and nutmeg

½ teaspoon ground cloves

½ cup (125ml) buttermilk

2 tablespoons golden syrup or treacle

20g (¾ ounce) glacé ginger, sliced thinly

lemon filling

125g (4 ounces) mascarpone cheese

125g (4 ounces) cream cheese, softened

¼ cup (40g) icing (confectioners') sugar

⅔ cup (160ml) thickened (heavy) cream

2 tablespoons lemon curd

lemon icing

¾ cup (120g) icing (confectioners') sugar

10g (½ ounce) butter, melted

1 tablespoon lemon juice

1 Preheat oven to 200°C/400°F. Grease and line oven trays with baking paper.

2 Beat butter, sugar and egg in small bowl with electric mixer until light and fluffy. Beat in sifted dry ingredients, buttermilk and golden syrup, in two batches, on low speed, until mixture is smooth.

3 Drop heaped teaspoons of mixture onto trays, about 4cm (1½ inches) apart.

4 Bake pies about 8 minutes. Cool on trays.

5 Meanwhile, make lemon filling and lemon icing.

6 Sandwich pies with filling. Drizzle icing over pies, top with glacé ginger.

lemon filling Beat cheeses and sugar in small bowl with electric mixer until smooth; beat in cream. Fold in curd for marbled effect.

lemon icing Combine sifted icing sugar and remaining ingredients in small bowl.

prep + cook time 55 minutes
makes 28

tip You can use bought lemon curd or lemon butter in this recipe or make your own. To make lemon curd, whisk 2 egg yolks and ¼ cup caster (superfine) sugar in small heatproof bowl until pale and thickened. Whisk in 1 teaspoon finely grated lemon rind and 2 tablespoons lemon juice; stir over small saucepan of simmering water about 12 minutes or until mixture coats the back of a spoon. Remove from heat; gradually whisk in 60g (2 ounces) chopped cold unsalted butter until combined between additions. Cover; refrigerate overnight.

WHITE CHOCOLATE PASSIONFRUIT POPCAKES

100g (3 ounces) unsalted butter, chopped coarsely

100g (3 ounces) white eating chocolate, chopped coarsely

½ cup (110g) caster (superfine) sugar

⅓ cup (80ml) milk

½ cup (75g) plain (all-purpose) flour

½ cup (75g) self-raising flour

1 egg, beaten lightly

¼ cup (60ml) passionfruit pulp

100g (3 ounces) white eating chocolate, melted

375g (12 ounces) white chocolate melts, melted

passionfruit icing

2 tablespoons passionfruit pulp

½ cup (80g) icing (confectioners') sugar

1 Preheat oven to 160°C/325°F. Grease 20cm x 30cm (8-inch x 12-inch) rectangular pan; line base with baking paper, extending paper 5cm (2 inches) over long sides.

2 Stir butter, chopped chocolate, sugar and milk in medium saucepan over low heat until smooth. Transfer mixture to medium bowl; cool 10 minutes. Whisk in sifted flours, then egg. Spread mixture into pan.

3 Bake cake about 30 minutes. Stand cake in pan 10 minutes before turning, top-side up, onto wire rack to cool.

4 Using hands, crumble the cake into large bowl; stir in passionfruit pulp and melted eating chocolate. Shape rounded tablespoons of mixture into balls, squeezing firmly; place on baking-paper-lined tray. Cover; refrigerate 4 hours.

5 Push one lollypop stick about half-way into each cake ball. Working quickly, dip cake balls in melted chocolate melts. Stand at room temperature until set.

6 Meanwhile, make passionfruit icing.

7 Spoon icing into piping bag fitted with small plain tube. Pipe icing over popcakes. Stand at room temperature until set.

passionfruit icing Strain passionfruit pulp through fine sieve into small bowl; discard seeds. Add sifted icing sugar; mix well.

prep + cook time
1 hour 10 minutes
(+ cooling & refrigeration)
makes 25
tips You need to press the cake mixture into balls using your hands – do not roll as the mixture will crumble. You will need 25 lollypop or paddle pop sticks for this recipe. When dipping the popcakes in chocolate, tilt the bowl of chocolate to one side, so the chocolate is deep enough to completely coat balls and a bit of the stick in chocolate, to endure the balls don't fall off the sticks. Push the sticks of the popcakes into the top of a cardboard egg carton to dry.

PUDDING ON A STICK

800g (1½ pounds) fruit cake
180g (5½ ounces) dark eating
   (semi-sweet) chocolate,
   melted
½ cup (125ml) brandy
½ cup (80g) icing
   (confectioners') sugar
9 glacé cherries (70g), quartered
royal icing
1½ cups (240g) pure icing
   (confectioners') sugar
1 egg white
½ teaspoon lemon juice

1 Using hands, crumble the cake into large bowl; stir in chocolate, brandy and sifted icing sugar. Using wet hands, roll rounded tablespoons of mixture into balls, pressing firmly; place on baking-paper-lined tray. Cover; refrigerate 4 hours.
2 Meanwhile, make royal icing.
3 Dip lollypop sticks into royal icing, then push sticks about half-way into cake balls.
4 Drizzle royal icing over cake balls, top each with a piece of cherry; stand at room temperature until set. Dust with a little extra sifted icing sugar.

royal icing Sift icing sugar through fine sieve. Lightly beat egg white in small bowl with electric mixer; beat in icing sugar, one tablespoon at a time. When icing reaches firm peaks, use a wooden spoon to beat in juice.

prep + cook time
1 hour 10 minutes (+ refrigeration)
makes 36
tips You will need 36 lollypop or paddle pop sticks for this recipe. We used a purchased 800g (1½-pound) fruit cake for this recipe; light or dark fruit cake is suitable, use whichever you prefer. Push the sticks of the popcakes into the top of a cardboard egg carton to dry.

CHOC CARAMEL MUD POPCAKES

100g (3 ounces) unsalted butter, chopped coarsely

100g (3 ounces) white eating chocolate, chopped coarsely

½ cup (110g) firmly packed dark brown sugar

⅓ cup (80ml) milk

1 tablespoon golden syrup or treacle

½ cup (75g) plain (all-purpose) flour

½ cup (75g) self-raising flour

1 egg, beaten lightly

180g (5½ ounces) white eating chocolate, melted

375g (12 ounces) milk chocolate melts, melted

1 tablespoon chocolate sprinkles

1 Preheat oven to 160°C/325°F. Grease 20cm x 30cm (8-inch x 12-inch) rectangular pan; line base with baking paper, extending paper 5cm (2 inches) over long sides.

2 Stir butter, chopped white chocolate, sugar, milk and golden syrup in medium saucepan over low heat until smooth. Transfer mixture to medium bowl; cool 10 minutes. Whisk in sifted flours, then egg. Spread mixture into pan.

3 Bake cake about 30 minutes. Stand cake in pan 10 minutes before turning, top-side up, onto wire rack to cool.

4 Using hands, crumble the cake into large bowl; stir in melted white chocolate. Shape rounded tablespoons of mixture into balls, squeezing firmly; place on baking-paper-lined tray. Cover; refrigerate 4 hours.

5 Push one lollypop stick about half-way into each cake ball. Working quickly, dip cake balls in melted milk chocolate, then sprinkle with chocolate sprinkles. Stand at room temperature until set.

prep + cook time
1 hour 10 minutes
(+ cooling & refrigeration)
makes 25
tips You need to press the cake mixture into balls using your hands – do not roll as the mixture will crumble. You will need 25 lollypop or paddle pop sticks for this recipe. When dipping the cake pops in melted chocolate, tilt the bowl of chocolate to one side, so the chocolate is deep enough to completely coat balls and a bit of the stick in chocolate; this will ensure the balls don't fall off the sticks. Push the sticks of the popcakes into the top of a cardboard egg carton to dry.

TIPS & TECHNIQUES

Classic puffs page 8
Place chopped butter and the water in saucepan. The butter must be finely chopped so that it melts quickly, before the water evaporates, which would upset the balance of the ingredients.

While the pan is still over the heat, add the flour all at once. Use a wooden spoon to quickly stir the ingredients together over the heat, until the mixture forms a ball and pulls away from the side and the base of the pan.

Transfer hot mixture to a medium heatproof bowl. Use a wooden spoon to beat in the eggs, one at a time, adding the last egg as required. For a three-egg recipe, beat in two eggs, keeping the last egg on the side.

Break the last egg into a cup, beat it with a fork. Gradually beat in enough of the egg until the mixture reaches the right consistency – it should be glossy and will gently fold over itself when the spoon is removed.

Pipe or spoon the pastry onto either greased oven trays, or greased trays that have been lined with baking paper; both work well. Leave about 5cm (2 inches) between each puff to allow for rising and spreading.

After the puffs are cooked, immediately cut a small slit in the bottom of each puff to allow the steam to escape. Use a piping bag, fitted with a plain piping tube, to pipe the filling through the slits in the puffs.

Paris brest page 11
Fit a piping bag with a large fluted tube; three-quarters fill the bag with pastry mixture. Pipe rings of pastry about 5.5cm (2¼ inches) in diameter and about 5cm (2 inches) apart, to allow for spreading and puffing.

Berry puff cheesecake page 19
Grease and line oven tray with baking paper. Three-quarters fill a large piping bag fitted with a large fluted tube with pastry mixture. Start from the outside of the circle, pipe inwards to make a spiral.

Valentine's croquembouche page 20
Fit a large piping bag with a plain tube (or without a tube); three-quarters fill the bag with pastry mixture. Hold the bag upright, pipe the pastry into 2cm (¾ inch) rounds.

Working quickly, use tongs or forks to dip the puffs one at a time into the toffee. The toffee is very hot and will conduct heat through metal, use heat resistant gloves or a cloth to protect your hands.

After one puff is toffee-dipped, place it onto a serving plate, add enough toffee-dipped puffs to make a circle; fill in the circle with more puffs. Stack more dipped puffs, one at a time, to form a cone shape.

Using two forks, dip the tines, up to about one-third of the length of the tines, into the remaining toffee. Quickly touch the tines of both forks together, then pull them apart to make fine strands of toffee over the puffs.

Gateau st honore page 23
Grease and line an oven tray with baking paper. Place round of puff pastry on tray. Fit a large piping bag with a large plain piping tube, fill bag with choux pastry. Pipe around edge of puff pastry.

Use remaining choux pastry to make puffs. Have crème patissiere at room temperature, spread or pipe crème patissiere evenly into baked pastry shape. Secure puffs to edge of pastry with a little toffee.

Fill centre of the gateau with strawberries – or any fresh fruit, drizzle with melted white chocolate. Dip the tines of two forks into toffee, quickly touch the tines together, pull them apart quickly, several times to make spun toffee.

Lemon curd & blueberry mille feuille page 41
Whisk egg yolks and sugar in heatproof bowl over pan of simmering water until pale; whisk in rind and juice until mixture coats the back of a spoon. Remove from heat, gradually whisk in butter.

Mini apple tarte tatins page 37
Roll dough, pulling gently into 20cm x 40cm (8-inch x 16-inch) rectangle. Fold down top third of the dough to cover another third of the dough; fold the bottom third up.

Give the dough a quarter turn, then re-roll into the same-sized rectangle as the last step. Fold the pastry into thirds as before. Enclose the pastry in plastic wrap; refrigerate the dough for 1 hour to allow it to rest.

Peel and quarter apples, shape into rounds to fit the pastry, using a cutter. Use a sharp vegetable knife to finely cut almost through the apple quarters. Keep apples in acidulated water until ready to use.

Apricot pastries page 45
Grease and line two oven trays with baking paper. Cut out rounds from pastry, place on trays. Use a 5cm (2-inch) cutter to mark the pastry, but do not cut all the way through.

Use a fork to prick the middle of the pastry rounds. Spread a level teaspoon of crème pâtissière into the centre of each round. Top each with a well-drained canned apricot half. Brush the pastry with a little beaten egg.

Snow eggs with blackberry fool page 74
Make snaps one at a time – this gives you time to handle and shape each one. Use the base of a small greased bowl or the silicone egg poacher mould we used for making the snow eggs.

Fill the silicone egg poaching moulds with the meringue mixture, carefully lift the moulds into a large wide shallow pan about half-full of simmering water. We cooked two at a time, but more can be cooked together.

Carefully lift the moulds from the water, turn them upside down onto a baking paper-lined tray. Gently turn the moulds inside out to release the snow eggs. These can be cooked several hours before you need them.

Lemon meringue pie page 73
Spoon the lemon filling into the cooked, cooled pastry case; spread the filling out evenly, covering the base completely and taking it to the edge of the pastry case.

Use a fork to roughen the surface of the filling. Spread meringue evenly over the filling, taking it to the edge of the pastry to seal. This will help the filling hold the meringue in position. Bake only until meringue is brown lightly.

White chocolate & passionfruit marshmallow biscuits page 77
Working with three at a time, spread biscuits with a little melted chocolate to secure marshmallows. Slide marshmallows out of pan, position on biscuits.

Half-fill a piping bag with the remaining melted white chocolate; pipe chocolate over top of marshmallows. Leave to set at room temperature.

Tropical french macaroons page 58
Grease and line oven tray with baking paper. Fit a large piping bag with a large plain piping tube (or without a tube). Hold the bag upright, pipe rounds onto tray, about 5cm (2 inches) apart.

Tap the tray on the bench to make the macaroon mixture spread slightly Stand the macaroons at room temperature for about 30 minutes or until they feel dry to touch.

Raspberry meringues with rosewater cream page 66
Spoon meringue onto baking-paper-lined tray into 12 freeform shapes about 5cm (2 inches) apart. Bake in very slow oven until meringues feel dry to touch.

Choc malt meringues page 78
Fit a large piping bag with a small plain tube; three-quarters fill bag with meringue mixture. To pipe flat meringues, pipe in small spiral shapes, holding the tube close to the paper while piping.

GLOSSARY

almonds
blanched whole nuts with the brown skins removed.
flaked paper-thin slices.
ground also known as almond meal.
baking paper also called parchment paper; a silicone-coated paper that is primarily used for lining baking pans and oven trays so cakes and biscuits won't stick, making removal easy.
bicarbonate of soda (baking soda) a raising agent used in baking.
butter use salted or unsalted (sweet) butter; 125g is equal to one stick (4 ounces) of butter.
buttermilk originally the term given to the slightly sour liquid left after butter was churned from cream, today it is made from no-fat or low-fat milk to which specific bacteria cultures have been added. Despite its name, it is actually low in fat.
cachous also called dragées; minuscule metallic-looking-but-edible confectionery balls; available in silver, gold or various colours.
cardamom a spice native to India; can be purchased in pod, seed or ground form. Has a distinctive aromatic and sweetly rich flavour.
cheese
cream commonly known as Philadelphia or Philly, a soft cow's-milk cheese with a fat content of at least 33%. Sold at supermarkets in bulk or in smaller-sized packages.
mascarpone an Italian fresh cultured-cream product made similarly to yogurt. Whiteish to creamy yellow in colour, with a buttery-rich, luscious texture. Soft, creamy and spreadable, it is used in Italian desserts and as an accompaniment to fresh fruit.

cherries, glacé also called candied cherries; boiled in a heavy sugar syrup then dried.
chocolate
dark eating (semi-sweet) also called luxury chocolate; made of a high percentage of cocoa liquor and cocoa butter, and a little added sugar.
melts small discs of compounded milk, white or dark chocolate ideal for melting and moulding.
milk eating the most popular eating chocolate, mild and very sweet; similar to dark with the difference being the addition of milk solids.
white eating contains no cocoa solids but derives its sweet flavour from cocoa butter. Is very sensitive to heat, so watch carefully when melting.
cinnamon dried inner bark of the shoots of the cinnamon tree; available in stick (quill) or ground form.
cloves dried flower buds of a tropical tree; can be used whole or in ground form. Has a distinctively pungent and 'spicy' scent and flavour.
cocoa powder also known as cocoa; dried, unsweetened, roasted then ground cocoa beans (cacao seeds).
dutch a richly flavoured dark coloured cocoa; available in specialist food stores and delicattesens.
coconut
cream obtained commercially from the first pressing of the coconut flesh alone, without the addition of water. Available from most supermarkets.
desiccated concentrated, dried, unsweetened and finely shredded coconut flesh.
extract synthetically produced from flavouring, oil and alcohol.
flaked dried flaked coconut flesh.

cornflour (cornstarch) available made from 100% corn (maize) or wheat; used as a thickening agent.
cream
pouring also called fresh or pure cream. It has no additives and a minimum fat content 35%.
thick (double) a dolloping cream with a minimum fat content of 45%.
thickened (heavy) a whipping cream containing a thickener; has a minimum fat content 35%.
custard powder instant mixture used to make pouring custard; it is similar to North American instant pudding mixes.
essence/extract an essence is either a distilled concentration of a food quality or an artificial creation of it. Coconut and almond essences are synthetically produced. An extract is made by extracting the flavour from a food product. In the case of vanilla, pods are soaked, usually in alcohol, to capture the authentic flavour. Essences and extracts keep indefinitely if stored in a cool dark place.
flour
plain (all-purpose) unbleached wheat flour, is the best for baking: the gluten content ensures a strong dough, which produces a light result.
self-raising plain flour that has been sifted with baking powder in the proportion of 1 cup flour to 2 teaspoons baking powder.
strong baker's also known as gluten-enriched, baker's or bread-mix flour. Produced from a variety of wheat that has a high gluten (protein) content and is best suited for pizza and bread making. It is available from supermarkets and health food stores.

food colouring dyes that can be used to change the colour of various foods; are edible and do not change the taste to a noticeable extent.

gelatine if using gelatine leaves, three teaspoons of powdered gelatine (8g or one sachet) is roughly equivalent to four gelatine leaves.

ghee clarified butter; with the milk solids removed, this fat has a high smoking point so can be heated to a high temperature without burning.

ginger
glacé fresh ginger root preserved in sugar syrup; crystallised ginger (sweetened with cane sugar) can be substituted if rinsed with warm water and dried before using.
ground also called powdered ginger; used as a flavouring but cannot be substituted for fresh ginger.

glucose syrup also known as liquid glucose, made from wheat starch; used in jam and confectionery making. Available at health food stores and supermarkets.

golden syrup a by-product of refined sugarcane; pure maple syrup or honey can be substituted.

hazelnuts, ground hazelnuts ground into a coarse or fine powder; also known as hazelnut meal.

liqueurs
cherry-flavoured we use kirsch.
hazelnut-flavoured we use frangelico.

malted milk powder a combination of wheat flour, malt flour and milk, which are evaporated to give the powder its fine appearance and to make it easily absorbable in liquids.

marzipan made from ground almonds, sugar and glucose. Similar to almond paste but is not as strong

in flavour; is finer in consistency and more pliable. Cheaper brands often use ground apricot kernels and sugar.

mixed spice a blend of ground spices usually consisting of allspice, cinnamon and nutmeg.

nutmeg a strong and pungent spice from the dried nut of a native Indonesian evergreen tree. Usually found ground, the flavour is more intense when freshly grated from the whole nut (available from spice shops).

oil
cooking spray we use a cholesterol-free spray made from canola oil.
vegetable any of a number of oils sourced from plant rather than animal fats.

orange blossom water also called orange flower water; concentrated flavouring made from orange blossoms. Available from Middle-Eastern food stores, delicatessens and some supermarkets. Can't be substituted with citrus flavourings as the taste is completely different.

pastry
fillo paper-thin sheets of raw pastry; brush each sheet with oil or melted butter, stack in layers, then cut and fold as directed.
sheets packaged ready-rolled sheets of frozen puff and shortcrust pastry, available from supermarkets.

peppermint extract is distilled from the essential oils of peppermint leaves. Commonly used in cooking.

rhubarb a plant with long, green-red stalks; becomes sweet and edible when cooked.

rosewater extract made from crushed rose petals; used for its aromatic quality in many sweetmeats

and desserts. Don't confuse with rose essence, which is more concentrated.

sugar
caster (superfine) also called finely granulated table sugar.
dark brown a moist, dark brown sugar with a rich, distinctive, full flavour coming from natural molasses syrup.
demerara a granulated, golden coloured sugar with a distinctive rich flavour; often used to sweeten coffee.
icing (confectioners') also known as powdered sugar; granulated sugar crushed together with a little added cornflour (cornstarch).
icing pure (confectioners') also known as powdered sugar, but has no added cornflour (cornstarch).
light brown an extremely soft, finely granulated sugar retaining molasses for its characteristic colour and flavour.
pearl also called nib or hail sugar; a product of refined white sugar, it is very coarse, hard, opaque white, and doesn't melt during baking. Available from specialist food stores.
white (granulated) also called crystal sugar; coarse, granulated table sugar.

sweetened condensed milk milk from which 60% of the water has been removed; the remaining milk is then sweetened with sugar.

treacle a concentrated, refined sugar syrup with a distinctive flavour and dark black colour.

vanilla
bean dried, long, thin pod from a tropical golden orchid; the minuscule black seeds inside the bean are used to impart a luscious vanilla flavour.
extract obtained from vanilla beans infused in water; a non-alcoholic version of essence.

INDEX

CONVERSION CHART

measures

One Australian metric measuring cup holds approximately 250ml; one Australian metric tablespoon holds 20ml; one Australian metric teaspoon holds 5ml.

The difference between one country's measuring cups and another's is within a two- or three-teaspoon variance, and will not affect your cooking results. North America, New Zealand and the United Kingdom use a 15ml tablespoon.

All cup and spoon measurements are level. The most accurate way of measuring dry ingredients is to weigh them. When measuring liquids, use a clear glass or plastic jug with metric markings.

We use large eggs with an average weight of 60g.

dry measures

METRIC	IMPERIAL
15g	½oz
30g	1oz
60g	2oz
90g	3oz
125g	4oz (¼lb)
155g	5oz
185g	6oz
220g	7oz
250g	8oz (½lb)
280g	9oz
315g	10oz
345g	11oz
375g	12oz (¾lb)
410g	13oz
440g	14oz
470g	15oz
500g	16oz (1lb)
750g	24oz (1½lb)
1kg	32oz (2lb)

liquid measures

METRIC	IMPERIAL
30ml	1 fluid oz
60ml	2 fluid oz
100ml	3 fluid oz
125ml	4 fluid oz
150ml	5 fluid oz
190ml	6 fluid oz
250ml	8 fluid oz
300ml	10 fluid oz
500ml	16 fluid oz
600ml	20 fluid oz
1000ml (1 litre)	32 fluid oz

length measures

3mm	⅛in
6mm	¼in
1cm	½in
2cm	¾in
2.5cm	1in
5cm	2in
6cm	2½in
8cm	3in
10cm	4in
13cm	5in
15cm	6in
18cm	7in
20cm	8in
23cm	9in
25cm	10in
28cm	11in
30cm	12in (1ft)

oven temperatures

The oven temperatures in this book are for conventional ovens; if you have a fan-forced oven, decrease the temperature by 10-20 degrees.

	°C (CELSIUS)	°F (FAHRENHEIT)
Very slow	120	250
Slow	150	300
Moderately slow	160	325
Moderate	180	350
Moderately hot	200	400
Hot	220	425
Very hot	240	475